The
Little Book
of Colour

The
Little Book
of Colour

How to Use the Psychology of Colour to
Transform Your Life

Karen Haller

PENGUIN LIFE

AN IMPRINT OF

PENGUIN BOOKS

PENGUIN LIFE

UK | USA | Canada | Ireland | Australia
India | New Zealand | South Africa

Penguin Life is part of the Penguin Random House
group of companies whose addresses can be found at
global.penguinrandomhouse.com.

First published 2019
001

Copyright © Karen Haller, 2019

The moral right of the author has been asserted

Designed by Hampton Associates
Printed in Italy by Printer Trento srl
Colour reproduction by Altaimage Ltd

A CIP catalogue record for this book is available from the British Library

ISBN: 978–0–241–35285–4

To Mama and Papa, thank you for giving me the freedom
to be fearless, curious, adventurous, brave
and above all to be my true self.

Contents

INTRODUCTION:

Colour – a language
we all speak

Toto, I have a feeling we're not in Kansas any more. I love this moment. Doesn't everyone love this moment? The wooden house has stopped spinning through the air and has crash-landed on the Wicked Witch of the East. Dorothy has brushed herself off and picked up her basket. With her little dog under her arm and her eyes wide as saucers, she's stepped from sepia into Technicolor. We can all see she's not in Kansas any more, but I love it that Dorothy says she *feels* it. There's the sparkling blue river, the lilac hills and huge pink flowers. And there's the Yellow Brick Road that will take her, the Scarecrow, the Tin Man and the Lion all the way to the Emerald City, where each will find what they've been searching for. This, in other words, is a story of personal transformation, a quest for self-discovery – and tell me if I'm wrong, but isn't it a story about colour too?

Colour is an amazing phenomenon. It is around us all the time and influences everything we do – though we are barely aware that this is happening. In fact, we are only around 20 per cent conscious of the colour decisions that we make, though we are making them all the time: about what we wear, what we eat, what we buy, how we relax, right down to how we take our morning cup of coffee. We have only to imagine doing without colour for a moment to see how much we rely on it to guide us through our everyday lives. Without colour, how would we know if a flying insect is harmless or will sting us, if a road is safe to cross, or if food is ripe or poisonous?

And how would we know what path to take to lead us to ourselves? For when we connect to colour, we connect to what we feel. And when we connect to what we feel, we can start to connect to who we are. Colour comes in through our eyes, but it makes its way into our hearts. It is woven into our emotions and influences how we think and how we behave. If we were to switch off colour, we would switch off our feelings. We would lose our most innate and fundamental means of self-expression. In a world without colour, we would become strangers to each other and lose touch with who we really are.

So how does colour do all this?

Our true colours

I have been researching and working with colour for more than twenty years. I look at how colour makes us think and feel, and how we can use it to benefit our wellbeing. I work with architects, interior designers, product designers, personal stylists, hospitals and major brands, as well as with individuals – and I know that, to really understand how to use colour to its full effect, we need to look at how it influences us on mental, physical and emotional levels. The psychology of colour can take us to the authentic personality, whether of a business or a person. And when we uncover the colours that are at the very core of our DNA, *that's* when the magic happens.

I have always instinctively known that working with colour is a magical process. I vividly remember the excitement I felt aged four or five years old, sitting in front of crayons and pots of paints and wondering what I would make with all these different colours. But, after school, I drifted into IT and the far-from-colourful work as a project manager and business analyst; and it wasn't until later, in my twenties, when I was studying fashion design and millinery back in my native Australia, that I had my colour epiphany. I was pinning chocolate-brown feathers on to a teal-blue hat, and just seeing the impact of the colours together stopped me in my tracks. I thought: That's it! It's colour! I didn't know quite what it all meant, but I knew I had to find out.

So I set out to learn everything there was to know about colour. Taking the traditional route to begin with, I spent a year studying basic colour theory, which focuses on the 'colour wheel'. This is the arrangement of hues in a circle that shows the relationships between primary, secondary and tertiary colours. It was originally developed by Isaac Newton and was intended for use by artists. It is fascinating, and it has its uses – but for me the colour wheel only scratched the surface. I had a sense that colour went deeper than that, that it connected us to our moods, our feelings and our behaviour. I wanted to understand why we respond to colour in the way we do and what lies behind its power to impact on the way we feel. The colour wheel couldn't answer my questions about why we are attracted to certain colours and why we feel differently about colours in different contexts. Why you like yellow, but I don't, why you think of red as exciting and friendly, while I find it aggressive and demanding, why I liked orange yesterday but not today, why certain tones of blue look good on you, but don't suit me, and dozens more questions like these . . . and I wanted to find the answers!

My search took me on a course in child psychology, and one in interior design, and to every colour teacher I could find – until by chance I stumbled on a weekend workshop in the highly researched but little known discipline of applied colour psychology. This, at last, was the missing piece of the jigsaw – a science that helps us to understand the language of colour and the impact it has on how we think, how we feel and how we behave – and my burning questions finally began to be answered. Like Dorothy waking up in Oz, I'd stepped into a whole new world of colour alchemy, where magic can happen. All my searches had come together. I began to see the transformative power of colour and the way it can change living and working spaces, businesses and people's lives beyond what they think is possible. Colour is not just about decorating. It is arguably the simplest tool we have at our disposal to enhance positive emotions and increase wellbeing, and it can do all this in an instant. It can help us to feel more connected to ourselves and to the people around us. When we feel connected, we feel happier about who we are. And when we feel happier about who we are, we can begin to lead happier and more fulfilled lives.

Ever since I began to understand the mind-blowing world of colour, I have been on a mission to share with anyone who wants to listen just how fascinating, inspiring and life-changing colour can be. The kind of world I want to live in is one in which everyone loves colour, and no one is afraid of it, or uncertain of how to use it. I want to create a global colour revolution in which we are no longer oblivious to this marvel that surrounds us. I want everyone to be able to speak the language of colour fluently – and in this book I'm going to teach you how.

Colour as a way of life

I will share with you everything I have learnt. We will look at the science and the history of colour. I will show you how colour works, how we can associate colour with our personal memories, the power of its symbolism and how it affects our thoughts, our deepest feelings and our behaviour. I will teach you everything you need to know to use it to transform how you feel, how you think and what you do in your day-to-day life. As you go through this book, you will learn how to use it to boost your confidence and your self-expression, and to help you to thrive in every aspect of your life – from the bedroom to the boardroom and all the places in between.

When you love colour, it loves you back. The more you get to know it, the more it will enhance your life and uplift your soul. I want this book to be your bedside colour bible, to be picked up and dipped into, for you to be inspired by and to learn from, whether you want to use colour to put outfits together with ease, create harmonious and beautiful spaces, help your focus and happiness at work, improve your relationships or just feel better in the moment.

Living a colourful life doesn't mean dressing top to toe in a kaleidoscope of colour – unless that's your thing of course! It's about being true to yourself and expressing who you really are. And we are all of us colourful, even the most quiet and subtle of us.

So, if you are ready to use the power of colour to learn about yourself, then come along with me. I will show you how to find what is right for you, in order to express your true self and your emotions, no matter what those colours might be. There are millions of colours out there in unique combinations just for you. It's time to paint your life with colour, and the world is your palette!

CHAPTER 1

The history of colour: an overview

Colour is one of life's great mysteries

E very culture and civilization has wondered about it. From the earliest humans to the present day, it has fascinated and perplexed us, amazed and delighted us.

But what exactly is it (apart from a phenomenon that most of us are blessed to see every day)? In this chapter, we will be looking at what makes the rainbow and the three things human beings need to be able to see colour. I will take you back to the beginnings of time to look at the development of our colour vision and to see how it evolved as part of a broad sensory and emotional experience. We will look at the natural world and discover that, when it comes to colour and how we use it, we are not so different from other living creatures after all. And I will take you through the history of the psychology of colour, from its earliest stirrings 2,500 years ago right up to today, where we stand on the cusp of a brand-new paradigm.

How do we see colour?

Light

In one sense, this question is easy to answer. Colour is simply just light. The colours we see are wavelengths of light that travel to us from the sun.

One way to think of wavelengths is like waves in the ocean. They are sometimes shorter and more frequent, and sometimes higher and more spread out. Each colour has its own particular wavelength and frequency, so the different colours we see are just different wavelengths of light coming at different rates. When all the waves are seen together, they make white light; so white light is actually made of all the colours of the rainbow because it contains all the different wavelengths.

The first person to understand what makes the rainbow was Isaac Newton, who discovered that when he shone sunlight through a glass prism he could break colour into its component parts.

He divided this array into seven colours – red, orange, yellow, green, blue, indigo and violet – and called his rainbow the 'colour spectrum', from the Latin *spectrum* 'image, apparition', from *specĕre*, 'to look, to see'. He chose seven colours because of the Ancient Greek belief in a connection between colours, musical notes, the solar system and the days of the week.

The colour spectrum ranges from dark red at 700 nanometres to violet at 400 nanometres (a nanometre is one thousand-millionth of a metre). And it is the only part of the sun's energy that we can see. Other forms of electromagnetic radiation include radio waves, gamma rays, X-rays and microwaves. It wasn't until the nineteenth century that the waves came to be measured, and light outside the visible range was discovered. Just beyond red is infrared, which we experience as heat, and just beyond violet is ultraviolet, which some birds, bees and other insects can see; this is what helps them to find nectar in flowers.

It is truly incredible that visible light is such a tiny part of the entire electromagnetic spectrum, and yet we can see millions of colours!

Reflected light

At the time of Newton's experiments in the late 1660s, people believed that colour was a mixture of light and darkness, and that prisms were what made light coloured – which brings us to the next piece in the colour-phenomenon puzzle.

What Newton demonstrated was that colour is, in fact, a property of the light reflected from objects, not a property of the objects themselves. When we look at an object, the colour we see depends on the light that is reflected from its surface into our eyes. Objects appear differently coloured because they absorb some wavelengths of light and reflect others. Our eyes only see those colours that are bounced off – or reflected.

White objects appear white because they reflect all colours. Black objects absorb all colours, so no light is reflected – which is one reason why it is uncomfortable to wear black clothes on a sunny day.

When I was learning about colour, this was the bit I found mind-blowing – and at times it still amazes me, that the colour we see is the colour that's being rejected. Imagine all the colours of the visible spectrum hitting these red apples, for example. We see them as red because the red light that each apple hasn't taken in is what is reflected back to us. All the other wavelengths have been absorbed.

Eyes

So we need light, a surface or an object for the light to be reflected off; and the final thing we need to experience colour is our eyes.

The sensation that we know as colour is our brain's interpretation of the signals coming from our eyes when light enters them. This is why we don't see colours in the dark. Colour is a product of how our eyes interpret light. Technically, you could say that colour doesn't exist. It is created only when our brain tries to interpret the light signals it receives.

Although we can distinguish the differences between 17 million colours, we are actually capable of detecting only green, red and blue lights. We do this through our photoreceptors. We have two types of photoreceptors in our eyes: rods and cones. The rods are responsible for our vision in low light (night vision) and the cones are responsible for picking up and processing higher levels of light – and our colour vision. We have three types of cones at the back of our eyes that are colour, or wavelength, specific. We have a cone for long waves of light (reds), a cone for shorter waves of light (blues) and a cone for in-between lengths (greens). All the millions of other colours we see are the result of these three types of cones working together and our brain interpreting their signals.

Did you know that dogs can't see many colours? This is because they have only two types of cones in their eyes rather than three. That one extra cone gives humans the ability to see millions more colours. How amazing is that?

Why do we see colour?

There is nowhere that has light that colour does not exist, but, until about 30 million years ago, our primitive mammalian ancestors had little use for it. They were nocturnal creatures and needed to see only what they could see in the dark. Once our vision had evolved to include the full spectrum of visible light, however, colour became our primary signalling language, and our ability to distinguish millions of colours every time we opened our eyes was a vital element in our survival. It helped us to find food, attract mates and avoid danger of every type. This instinctive and subconscious understanding of colour's coded messages is at the very centre of our existence.

We have only to look at other living creatures to see how this works. Darwin suggested there were three main uses of colour in the natural world.

Attraction. For a species to survive, it must mate. One of the main ways colour is used is to attract a mate. Birds do this to great effect. The male bird will display its brightly coloured plumage and do a dance and sing a song to court a mate.

Protection: Camouflage. From stick insects that turn green to blend in with a blade of grass, to the pigmy seahorse that turns the same colour red as the coral it lives in, animals use colour to protect themselves and hide from predators.

They also use colour to increase their chances of sneaking up on their prey without being seen. The immediate environment determines what colour or colours they have evolved in which to camouflage themselves. Think of the Arctic fox, for example, which turns white in winter to blend in with the snow.

Protection: Warning. While some animals choose to hide, others use colour to shout out a warning: come near me at your peril!

In nature, yellow, orange and red can signal danger. As the colours go up the scale, the danger signal intensifies. Orange is more toxic than yellow, and red is more toxic than orange. A further danger signal is created when black is added to these colours. You wouldn't want to go near the redback spider in Australia, which is coloured red and black. And we all know that a yellow-and-black flying insect will sting us.

Then there are the mimickers – those animals that use these colours to pretend that they are poisonous or to be something they are not in order to protect themselves. The harmless hoverfly mimics the venomous hornet in colouring as a form of protection against would-be predators.

Our colour understanding today may be much more subconscious than it was for our early ancestors, but we still have absolute instinctive reactions to colour – and those reactions can be just as powerful as they ever were. We respond to the colours in the world around us today as we once responded to the colours in the natural environment in which we lived. We still understand the messages that colour sends us – and we still use colour to attract a mate, or to hide or to protect ourselves, as we will see in Chapter 4.

Not just something we see

But it doesn't stop there – and this is where things get really interesting.

When light enters our eyes, striking a cone, it triggers the release of a chemical transmitter, initiating electrical messages that are conveyed to the brain and eventually the hypothalamus. The hypothalamus, together with the pituitary gland – a pea-sized structure at the base of our brain – governs our:

- metabolism
- appetite
- body temperature
- water regulation
- sleep
- autonomic nervous system
- sexual and reproductive functions

What that means is that colour isn't just a visual stimulus. It also creates physiological changes within us. In psychological terms, it delivers an emotional experience.

I can actually see this happen to the audience during my talks. I start by projecting a series of black-and-white images on to a screen. After a minute or two I switch to colour. The same images are up on the screen, but this time the fields are green, the banana is yellow, the bird is blue. When the black-and-white images are up, everyone just sits there, slumped and staring. But when I switch to colour, they all straighten up. They breathe out, their shoulders relax, their faces change. They feel that emotional connection, and it registers in their whole body.

Established research into theories of colour and psychology suggests that each colour has specific effects that influence us on all levels – emotional, mental and physical. In other words, different wavelengths of light trigger different feelings. In Chapter 3 we will see how different colours can excite or depress, calm or re-energize, make us feel angry or happy, warm or cool, hungry or tired. Every colour signal creates an impact. Every colour affects how we think, how we feel and how we behave.

The psychology of colour: a brief history

Empedocles *c.*490–*c.*430 BC

Although the idea of linking colour to four personality types (see Carl Jung, p. 31) was still a couple of thousand years off, it has its basis all the way back in the work of the philosopher Empedocles, who divided matter into the four elements of nature: Fire, Earth, Air and Water. He called these four elements 'roots' and believed that it was from these roots that all things, including all living creatures, are created. The analogy he liked to use was to compare creating life with painting. Life springs from a mixture of these four elements, he said, in just the same way that a painter can create a whole world from just a few colours.

Hippocrates 460–370 BC

The father of modern medicine, the Greek physician Hippocrates, moved this thinking on with his theory of the four bodily fluids. The four fluids were referred to as the four humours, from the Latin word *hūmor*, meaning 'bodily fluid' or 'discharge'. They were: Blood, Yellow Bile, Black Bile and Phlegm. He linked each humour with each of the four elements: Fire, Earth, Air and Water.

Hippocrates believed that we are all born with a mixture of these four humours, and that each humour had to be balanced according to one's temperament. An imbalance of bodily fluids was what caused illness or unhappiness.

The humour theory became the most commonly held view of the human body among European doctors until the nineteenth century. Although Hippocrates's belief that one can determine a person's personality type from the proportions of their bodily fluids is no longer taken seriously, his behavioural observations were so accurate that they form the basis of many personality theories today.

Aristotle 384–322 BC

The first known theory of colour was developed by Aristotle, who believed that colour was sent as celestial rays of light by God from heaven. He associated colours with the four elements, Fire, Earth, Air and Water, and suggested that all colours came from white and black – that is, from light and the absence of it. In his view, blue and yellow were the true primary colours, since blue is the first colour we see when we look into the dark, and yellow is the first colour we see when we look towards the light.

He developed a linear colour system that ranged from white at midday to black at midnight. This was the way colours were arranged until Newton came along 2,000 years later.

Galen AD c.130–c.210

Like Hippocrates, the Greek physician Galen believed illness to be the result of an imbalance of the four humours and that the cure was to bring them back into balance. However, he went further in linking the excess of a particular humour with particular personality traits and the qualities of dry, wet, cold and hot. He called these traits 'temperaments' and named them: Sanguine (Blood), Choleric (Yellow Bile), Melancholic (Black Bile) and Phlegmatic (Phlegm).

Isaac Newton 1642-1727

Much of what we understand about light and colour comes from Newton, who, in 1666, solved the puzzle of the rainbow (some believe by accident!). He also gave us the first circular diagram for colour, taking the violet end of the spectrum and joining it up to the red. This arrangement puts the primary colours – red, yellow and blue – opposite their complementary colours, and shows that each can enhance the effect of the other through optical contrast. The colour opposite blue, for example, is orange. When you put these colours next to each other, it makes the blue look bluer and the orange seem even more orange. In this way, the effect was considered 'complementary', a term now mistakenly thought simply to mean the two colours look pleasing together. The colour wheel, as it became known, was an incredibly useful tool for artists, and its impact on the way colour is thought about and understood has lasted right up to today. It will be the first (and possibly only) thing you are taught if you study colour, as I discovered for myself when I embarked on my own colour journey.

Johann Wolfgang von Goethe 1749-1832

Newton's views on colour and light went relatively unchallenged until the great Romantic German poet and novelist Goethe published his 1,400-page treatise on colour in 1810. While Newton had understood colour as a physical phenomenon, Goethe saw it as an emotional experience that each of us perceives differently. He was fascinated by the way our brains process visual information and by the physiological effects that colour can have on us. He sought to discover laws of colour harmony and to define the ways in which certain colours can create certain feelings. With Goethe's doctrine of colours, we enter into the world of modern colour psychology.

Carl Jung 1875-1961

The most prominent thinker in the field of colour psychology is the Swiss psychiatrist Carl Jung. Building on the work of Hippocrates, Jung divided the four temperaments into personality types in relation to colour and used them to explain the inner motivations of human behaviour.

- Cool Blue: showing no bias, objective, detached, analytical
- Earth Green: still, tranquil, calming, soothing
- Sunshine Yellow: cheerful, uplifting, spirited, enthusiastic
- Fiery Red: positive, decisive, bold, assertive

Jung saw that there were positive and negative aspects in each of the four temperaments and surmised that, while we all contain something of each of them, the proportions will vary with the individual and that we are likely to connect to one colour energy in particular.

Bauhaus 1919-33

I'm a big fan of the Bauhaus, the visionary school of art in Germany set up by the architect Walter Gropius in 1919 that aimed to bring together art, design, craft and industry in one artistic association. Gropius looked for radical, modern thinkers to teach the students, and two of the most inspiring were Wassily Kandinsky and Johannes Itten.

Kandinsky's colour theory, published in 1911, aimed to explain how a painter chooses a particular palette: either by the effect it has on the eye, or by its psychological effect – the way in which the painter connects emotionally with the colours. 'Every colour is inwardly beautiful in painting because every colour creates a spiritual vibration and every vibration enriches the soul.'

Itten considered colour to have an energy that affects us either positively or adversely, and his interest lay in the connections between colour and emotions, and colour and shapes. He attributed qualities like warm and cool to describe how colours react with each other and how they are likely to affect people both physically and psychologically. He noticed how his students favoured certain tones of colours and believed there was a correlation between a student's personality and self-expression in their work and the tonal colour palette they favoured.

Itten was the first to associate colour palettes with four types of personality and to assign one personality type to each of the four seasons.

Angela Wright 1939-

Taking the colour personality theories of Carl Jung and the great minds before her a step further, Angela Wright, in the 1970s, developed a unified theory of colour psychology and colour harmony to explore how colour affects how we feel, think and behave. The seven basic tenets of the Colour Affects System are:

1. Each hue affects distinct psychological states
2. The psychological effects of colour are universal
3. Every shade, tone or tint can be classified into one of four colour groups
4. Every colour will harmonize with every other colour in the same group
5. All humanity can be classified into one of four personality types
6. Each personality type has a natural affinity with one colour group
7. Response to colour schemes is influenced by personality type

This is the basis of applied colour psychology. With this combination of the science of colour harmony and the study of human psychology, we took a huge step forward in our understanding of the impact colour has on us and how it can be used to shape behaviour.

The evolution of colour: colour today

The Bauhaus was closed down by Hitler in 1933 and ways of thinking about colour changed with the Second World War. In a world of rationing, loss and hardship, it came to be seen as unnecessary and frivolous. It was pushed to the sidelines as a luxury, its intrinsic connection to our emotions forgotten about. In the following decades, insofar as it was thought about at all, colour was considered merely aesthetic, a decorative afterthought – not as integral to design, and certainly not to our wellbeing.

But here's another amazing thing about colour. It is not this fixed thing that is out there in the world and that's that. It is constantly evolving. As we evolve and develop, so too does the way we use and interact with colour – and we are by no means at the end of our colour journey. In fact, we are entering a whole new phase. Everywhere I look, I see people embracing colour, becoming more conscious of its impact. We drive more colourful cars, we dye our hair more colourful hues, our shops are full of more colourful products. Colour is an increasingly important topic of consideration for neuroscientists, biologists, physicists, philosophers and psychologists; and research is continually expanding our knowledge of how we take colour in and how we emotionally respond to it.

Harnessing our emotional connection to colour is what this new paradigm is all about – and is at the very heart of all the work I do. Like the Bauhaus before me, I look for ways to bring colour not just to the core of design but to the centre of our lives, to embrace the power it has to influence our behaviour for the better, to create positive states of wellbeing and to help us thrive – to revolutionize both the way we see it and the way we use it.

Through my experience over many years, I have found that there are three main ways we relate to colour:

1. *Personal colour association.* This is a largely conscious association we have made between a particular hue, or tone of colour, and something personal to us, like the colours of our favourite football team, or a colour associated with a memory, like the colour of your great-grandma's cardigan. We will see how this works in detail in Chapter 4.

2. *Cultural or symbolic meaning.* This is usually a deeply imbedded belief about a colour within a culture. A colour may have gained symbolic significance over many generations, if not hundreds of years, and slipped into folklore, as we will see in Chapter 2.

3. *Psychological meaning.* When we see colour, we understand the messages it sends on a largely unconscious level. Colour speaks to us in a language we understand instinctively – the language of emotions – and it influences our behaviour without our necessarily being aware of it. We will see more of this in Chapter 2.

As we go through the book, you will see how to uncover these responses in yourself, to peel back the layers and bring what has long lain hidden into the light of day. Understanding how we relate to colour is the key to every colour decision we make. The more conscious we become of our colour choices, the better we will be able to use colour to create the positive outcomes we want. This is why I get so excited about applied colour psychology. The more people have this incredible tool in their tool box, the more we can create homes, office spaces, shops, restaurants, healthcare facilities, schools and universities that are able to use colour with purpose to encourage positive feelings and behaviours – and the closer we can get to taking the next big step in colour's evolutionary progress.

CHAPTER 2

Perceiving colour

Do you see what I see?

When I sat down at a meeting with the publishers of this book, one of the team brought out a swatch of colour to discuss. I saw it as a light aqua green. She saw a light blue. And someone else described it as turquoise. We each saw the colour differently – what I called aqua green was called something different by everyone at the table. I have this conversation every time I sit down with people to talk about colour, but none of us is 'right' or 'wrong'. The label each of us gives a colour can depend on our experience of it, the quality of the light shining when we see it, how often we have seen it, and how much we have been exposed to it. I was once stopped by a lady in a department store having a heated discussion with her husband over by a clothes rail. 'My husband and I are having a debate over this colour,' she said. 'He thinks it's navy blue and I think it's periwinkle blue. Which of us is right?' Of course, she had no idea I was a colour specialist and got a bit of a surprise when I was able to see the argument from both sides. I said that I agreed with them both. It was blue. It was a dark blue. It's just that they had different names for it. He labelled it navy and she labelled it periwinkle. I suspected that, unlike her husband, she'd had exposure to the variation of blue she called periwinkle, and that was what had led her to give the tone a more nuanced name.

It is fascinating that we can each of us look at the same colour and yet describe it completely differently. What colour do you think the circle opposite is? If you show it to someone else, what colour name do they give it?

Interestingly, research has shown that women and men do indeed see colour differently, and that, while men are good at seeing fast-moving shapes from a distance, women are better at distinguishing subtle gradations of colour close up. This is particularly noticeable with colours that lie in the middle of the spectrum. Women are able to distinguish varieties of yellow and green that look identical to men, and men require slightly longer wavelengths of light to be able to see the same tints, tones and shades as women.

Now why should this be? One possible explanation goes back to our earliest existence. According to anthropologists, men developed the ability to distinguish between predators and prey from a distance, while women evolved the skills that enabled them to search out food and to know if it was safe to eat. Let's remember why we developed colour vision in the first place. Colour vision facilitates what scientists call 'contrast detection'. If you have colour vision, you are much better at seeing something against a background, like fruit in a tree or berries in a bush. If you weren't good at this back in our hunter–gatherer days, you would go hungry. Or worse, of course. So women's chromatic sensitivity would have been vital to our survival as a species.

Scientists suspect that there is a small percentage of women among us today who have evolved an even greater colour sensitivity and might – theoretically at least – be able to see millions more colours than the average person. This comes down to the science of cones that we read about in the last chapter, the photoreceptors at the back of our eyes that send information to our brain to create the sensation of colour. Most people have three types of cones, or receptors, in their retinas, but some women are said to have a genetic mutation that means they have a fourth.

Let's take a moment to do the maths. Remember that the cones are wavelength – or colour – specific, and that each type of cone enables us to distinguish around 100 colours. For a person with three cones, each of those 100 colours will be multiplied by the power of three, to give at least a million different colours. If you have two types of cones, each colour will be multiplied by the power of two, to give 10,000 possible hues. But if you add a cone, that number increases by a factor of 100, allowing you – perhaps – to see around 100 million colours. A so-called tetrachromat (person with four types of cones) could look at a clear blue sky and see dozens of colours; a rainbow might contain hundreds of different hues; white light could be filled with blue white, yellow blue, violet grey, purple, pink, gold . . . a whole kaleidoscope of colours for which we don't have names (more on colour naming later).

So how do we know if we are tetrachromatic or not? I might be. You might be. Because the way that we perceive colour is a subjective experience, it is not easy for us to tell whether we have enhanced powers of colour perception or not. There are varying estimates of how many women across the world might carry this extra cone, but actually proving that they can see more colours than the rest of the population remains somewhat elusive.

At the opposite end of the scale from tetrachromacy is colour-vision deficiency, known as colour-blindness. This occurs when our light-sensitive cones fail to respond appropriately to the different wavelengths of light. Instead of reacting separately to each wavelength of light, the cones treat each wavelength somewhat similarly. Most people with colour-vision deficiency can see as clearly as other people, but the mixed-up messages of their retinal cones make it difficult for them to distinguish between colours, or to see them as brightly. This is why traffic lights are red at the top and green at the bottom, so that people who have a colour deficiency can tell from the position of the lights whether to stop or to go.

Colour-blindness is a relatively common condition, affecting approximately 1 in 12 men and 1 in 200 women in the UK. So it is quite likely that you may know a man with colour-vision deficiency, but it is also likely that he may not know himself that he is affected in this way. Because we have words and symbols to describe the world in addition to colour, people without full colour vision may not ever realize that they don't see the world in the array of hues that other people do. And, even if they are aware that they can't see the colours other people see, they cannot empirically know what they are missing – you can't give someone else the visual experience of the colour purple merely by explaining what purple is like for you.

Colour-correcting glasses

———

Did you know that there are now special glasses that can correct colour deficiency and enhance colour perception for some people?

The glasses work by rectifying the underlying cause of colour-blindness – the failure of the cones to distinguish between the wavelengths of light – and by amplifying the colour signal sent to the brain, so that colours look brighter and more saturated. Wearers of the glasses will see colours that they have never seen before and will notice details and differentiations that they would previously have overlooked. The world will appear richer and more vibrant. A real Dorothy in Oz experience!

I have seen people cry when they put these glasses on from the sheer joy of being able to see what the rest of us take for granted. It makes you realize what a gift it is, to be able to experience the phenomenon of colour.

For one fascinating group of people, colour perception is a whole multi-sensory experience, involving tastes, smells, sounds, shapes, words, music and textures. These people are called synaesthetes – from the New Latin *syn*, meaning 'together/union of', and *anæsthesia*, 'to feel, perceive' – and they have a kind of heightened sensitivity, whereby one sense, like hearing, is joined to another sense, such as sight. There are thought to be about sixty different types of synaesthesia, of which two of the most common are grapheme synaesthesia – seeing letters or numbers, whole words or days of the week as inherently coloured – and chromaesthesia – seeing colours when hearing music. Lots of artists and musicians claim to be synaesthetes – including the musician Pharrell Williams and the singer-songwriter Stevie Wonder.

The Bauhaus artist Wassily Kandinsky, whom we met in the last chapter, saw colours when he heard music and heard music when he painted; for him the association was so strong that each colour corresponded to an exact musical note. He is one of the first people known to have had synaesthesia, and he wrote a lot about what the experience felt like to him. For Kandinsky, colour was combined with both his sense of touch and his sense of smell, and I love what he said about the ability of some colours to create 'a feeling of satisfaction, of pleasure, like a gourmet who has a tasty morsel in his mouth'. Don't you just know what he means!

What I find most exciting is what he wrote about the different feelings that different colours give rise to, how colours can make you feel elated or depressed, energized or tired, bored or calm, satisfied or hopeless, disturbed or happy. In fact, his synaesthetic understanding of colours and how they can make us feel aligns with contemporary colour psychology. It's thought that, when he was young, Kandinsky said that 'Each colour lives a mysterious life of its own' – and we will see exactly what he means by that in Chapter 3.

What's in a name?

But, of course, it doesn't end there. There is a whole other chapter in the story of colour perception – and this has to do with language: that is, with the way we divide up the colour spectrum and the words we use to define its different elements. The question anthropologists and philosophers have long been asking is: do different cultures see colours differently? Is red still red in a different language?

In the English language, there are eleven basic terms for colour: red, pink, yellow, orange, brown, blue, green, purple, grey, white and black.

But it might surprise you to learn that not all languages classify colours in the same way. Some languages have more than eleven basic words for colour, and some languages have fewer. Russian and Greek, for example, have two words for blue, distinguishing light blue from dark blue in the way that, in English, we distinguish between red and pink. Hungarian uses two words to distinguish between darker red and lighter red. Hindi includes saffron as a basic colour but has no standard term for the colour grey. Indeed, many cultures don't have a word for the colour blue (in fact, blue is a relatively recent colour term in the English language), and actually use one term both for blue and for green interchangeably. The word for green is used to describe the colour of the sky in Vietnamese and Thai, and in Japanese a green traffic light is blue. (And we'll come back to this shortly.)

Some cultures have very few words for colour. For example, the Bassa people of Liberia classify colours into just two categories: *ziza* for red/orange/yellow and *hui* for green/blue/purple. The Shona tribe in South Africa divide colours into three: orange/red, yellow/green and blue/green. The Hanunó'o language, spoken in the Philippines, has four basic colour words: black, white, red and green. And some New Guinean languages, such as the Pirahã language, have terms only for black and white, or dark and light.

But do these differences mean that speakers of languages with fewer words for colour see less of it than speakers of languages with more terms? Research has indicated this is not necessarily the case, and that the very opposite might be true. The Himba tribe of Namibia, for example, is famous for being able to see dozens of nuances of green that appear the same to Western eyes, though they have only five words for colour in their language:

- *serandu* – reds, browns, oranges and some yellows
- *dambu* – a variety of greens, reds, beige and yellows
- *zuzu* – most dark colours, black, dark red, dark purple, dark blue
- *vapa* – some yellows and white
- *buru* – a variety of greens and blues

Take a look at the image on the right and see how quickly you can find the square that is a different shade of green.

Can you find it?

The two types of green on the previous page are labelled with two different Himba words – which means that the Himba people see them as two separate colours. Faced with this test, the Himba have no trouble seeing these shades of green as distinct and can quickly and easily pick out the odd square. On the other hand, in a similar test that had eleven green squares and one blue one, the Himba struggled to pick the odd square out, though to Western eyes it appears obvious. And it is thought that that's because the Himba group blue and green under the same term, and therefore find it hard to see them as distinct.

Nobody seems to know quite why different cultures divide the colour spectrum differently, but what these findings do suggest to researchers is that how we see colours is to a large degree dependent on the words that we have in our repertoire for them. And what that implies is that we may very well be seeing the world differently from the way our neighbours see it.

We may never be able really to know what people whose language has no word for a particular colour actually see when they describe the leaves on a tree, the flowers in a field or a cloudless sky. But one mystery that seems to have been solved is the order in which colour terms appear in a language. Anthropologists and linguists seem to agree that, if a language has only two terms, it will first distinguish between light and dark: light, as in white, and dark, as in black. If a language has a third term for colour, it will always be red. The fourth term is generally green, followed by yellow and then blue, with pink, purple, brown, grey and orange coming at various stages afterwards.

And this fixed order seems to be a result of how our eyes work. Yes, here's our old friend wavelength frequency again. According to scientists, the order in which we name colours matches our reaction to the different frequencies of visible light. Colours don't arise in a random fashion but emerge in accordance with the biology of how we see the world. We name long-wave light (red) first, then medium-wave light (green) and then short-wave light (blue).

The evolution of colour naming

What is fascinating to me is that the spectrum isn't fixed in its colour categories. Colour words, like other words, can evolve over time – and colour categories can expand. One wonderful example of this is how the Japanese developed their word for green – *midori*. Up until about the year 1000, the Japanese used one word both for green and for blue. This word was *ao*. Around the year 1000, another word emerged for the greenish end of blue – *midori*. But *midori* wasn't a colour in its own right. It was only a shade of *ao*. Then, in 1917, crayons began to be imported into the country, and the crayons made a distinction between blue and green in the colour spectrum. There were blue crayons and there were green crayons, and schoolchildren therefore began to give them separate names. *Midori* came into its own at last. Not everything was seamlessly reclassified, however. Some things just stuck with *ao* – and that is why a green traffic light in Japan is still called blue.

Likewise, the word for the colour orange didn't begin to appear in English until after the fruit was imported into Britain in the Middle Ages. The first recorded use of orange to refer to a colour was in 1512. Before then, if an English-speaking person wanted to refer to something orange coloured, they might have used the Old English word *geoluread*, which literally means yellow-red, or reached for the nearest word available. The robin red breast, red squirrel and red fox are all actually orange coloured, but what else were people to do when they had no word for orange yet?

The most recent basic colour term to come into existence in English is pink, which came into usage as a colour word in the early 1600s and meant a pale rose colour. Originally used as a verb, 'to pink' dates back to the fourteenth century and means 'to decorate with a perforated or punching pattern'; this is where we got the name for the zig-zag scissors we call 'pinking shears'. Pink is the name of a genus of flowers called *Dianthus*, and so named because its zig-zag petals look as though they have been cut with pinking shears.

The American anthropologist Brent Berlin and linguist Paul Kay introduced the eleven basic colour terms in their 1969 book *Basic Colour Terms: Their Universality and Evolution*. Berlin and Kay's work was met with acclaim, becoming widely accepted and leading to a new way of thinking about colour terms and colour naming. But colour, as you now know, is a living, breathing thing, and so it didn't just stop there. Whatever colour knowledge we have, there is always somebody somewhere building on it. And, in this case, there is a researcher based at University College London – Dimitris Mylonas – who is busy shining a light into those areas of colour that Berlin and Kay didn't look at: the colours that lie in between the eleven main colours, the parts of the rainbow where green blends into yellow, yellow blends into orange, and orange into red, and so on.

As Dimitris explained it to me when I visited his laboratory, colour is continuous. One colour doesn't abruptly stop and then another start; they blend into each other. Colour is a continuum, and how do you divide a continuum into distinct categories? Dimitris wants to discover what you call those colours between one hue and the next, which are neither one thing nor the other, those blends like the yellowish red we now call orange. For him, the basic eleven terms are simply not enough. 'I believe that colour names are like pencils,' he told me. 'The more colour names you have, the more colour you are going to use in your everyday life.'

Well, I couldn't agree more, of course, and so when he asked me if I would like to take part in his lab-controlled research, I agreed. First, Dimitris checked to see if I had any kind of colour deficiency, and then, in a dark room, on an extremely well-calibrated computer screen, I was shown around 600 different colours in quick succession and asked to give a name to each of them. These were the in-between colours – taupes and reddy browns, aqua greens, orangey pinks, purple blues – and I was amazed at how difficult I found it to attribute a known name to them all. I had the most names for the green shades like grass green, lime green, emerald, forest, olive, sage, mint and aqua, but I was very surprised by how few names I had for purple, other than the common ones such as lilac, lavender, aubergine, royal purple and mauve. When I had finished, I felt as if I had just run a colour-naming sprint!

While what I did was part of a laboratory-controlled experiment, thousands of people from across the world have been taking part in Dimitris's online version of the study since it launched at the end of 2007. For Dimitris, this shows that a lot of people feel just the same as he does about the inadequacy of the eleven basic colour terms to describe all colours and share his desire to improve the way we communicate with each other about colour. It also gives him a huge amount of data. What this data has revealed is that, in British English at least, the number of basic colour terms should be extended from eleven to thirteen, and that the two additional colour terms should be turquoise and lilac. Both these colours are large categories in themselves, he explained, and are easily identified by large numbers of people. They share similar characteristics with other basic colour terms, like red or orange, and improve the precision of colour naming. Whether or not turquoise and lilac will actually be accepted as basic colour terms is another matter. Not all researchers agree with Dimitris's findings and, as he explained, turquoise is a long word that many people find difficult to spell – which doesn't help its progress towards acceptance.

I have long felt that lime green (also known as chartreuse) should be included as a basic colour term, and I asked him what he thought. It's a good candidate, he agreed. But, like turquoise, lime green is slightly too cumbersome a term to catch on. It needs to lose the 'green' part and just become 'lime'. We are linguistically lazy, it turns out, and won't use long words if we don't have to, so our basic colour terms have to be snappy too.

Oh, and one more thing. I asked Dimitris if his research had revealed any differences between the way in which men and women differentiate nuances of colour. And he told me that, yes, it had. His findings in English, Spanish and Russian all showed that women have a richer colour vocabulary than men and use a larger number of colour terms. And why did he think that was? I asked. Women need more colour names, he said, because they use more colour. Now if only I'd been able to explain that to the arguing couple in the department store.

The meaning of colour in cultures

Just as we give colours names, so too we ascribe them meanings – and we have done this since the beginning of time. The recent discovery of what anthropologists describe as the world's oldest paint workshop, in the Blombos Cave on the Southern Cape coast of South Africa, shows that, as far back as 100,000 years, our most ancient ancestors were collecting pigment and mixing it into a paste. And, although we don't know precisely what these cave dwellers used their colour paste for – perhaps some sort of ritual practice – it seems clear that it meant something significant to them.

By the time of the Ancient Egyptians, we had six basic colours – black, white, red, green, blue and yellow – and each colour meant something specific. Colour was the basis of everything fundamental in Ancient Egypt, such as life, death, fertility, harvest and victory. In fact, their word for colour was used interchangeably with the word they used for 'character', 'being' or 'nature', so integral was colour to their worldview.

And is it so different today? We live and breathe in colour, and every culture and society has colours that mean something significant to them. Colour deepens the meanings of our traditions and rituals: we use it to mark our honours and achievements, to keep us safe, or to wish us luck, long life, prosperity, fertility, love or happiness. Colour is linked to our politics, our religions and our histories. It is part of the stories we tell ourselves about who we are and what we believe, what we are doing and where we are in the world.

The natural palette of a country has deep potency too and can carry powerful meanings for all of us, whether we live in a place or are just passing through. I've been travelling in one way or another – with family, friends, on sporting exchanges and as a solo adventurer – since I was five years old, and have been to more than seventy countries. When I close my eyes, it is always the colours that come back to me. Colour is our way of knowing a place. Walk through the markets of the world, and you will know where you are by the piles of brightly coloured spices or vibrant herbs, the baskets of fruits and vegetables, the buckets of salsas, the cloths, rugs, carpets and household wares, as well as by the local brick and stone and the colours of the paintwork.

My most memorable experiences of other countries are saturated in colour – sometimes quite literally. Like the time I had been trekking in the Himalayas, and came down from the mountains into Kathmandu just as the festival of Holi was taking place. During the two days of Holi, men, women and children take to the streets and drench each other with coloured powder and water. The air is painted in every colour of the rainbow, blues, yellows, greens, reds, violets and pinks, each one of which has a meaning in the

Indian psyche. I was working in IT at that time, and when I arrived in the UK from Holi I had to go to a job interview. But I couldn't get the colours out of my hair. I sat in that grey office, hair twisted and pinned up, desperately trying to hide all the colours, but still knowing they were there in all their glory. Perhaps the universe was trying to tell me something?

Colour can have different meanings depending on where you are in the world. If you ask, 'What does the colour red symbolize?', the answer will depend on which country you are in. A colour can mean one thing in one country and the exact opposite in another. Take white for example, which symbolizes purity in the West and is traditionally worn by brides to represent their virginity. In China and in some Asian countries, on the other hand, white represents death, mourning and sadness, and is traditionally worn at funerals.

I find it absolutely fascinating to look at the different meanings colours traditionally hold in different countries and the way this permeates every facet of life, from what people wear to what they eat, their daily rituals and grand ceremonies, on a personal level and across society.

World Colour Symbolism

White

In India, white is the colour worn for funerals. In the West, white symbolizes purity, innocence, goodness and peace. In China, it is the colour that represents death and mourning.

Black

The colour of mourning and loss in the West, but brides in Spain traditionally wear a black gown and lace mantilla to represent their devotion to their husband until death. In Africa, black is a symbol of experience and wisdom. In Japan, it is the colour of mystery and the night. It denotes non-being. It can also represent anger. In India, a black dot is placed on a newborn baby's face to ward off the evil eye.

Red

In South Africa red symbolizes the bloodshed of the Apartheid Era and has come to be seen as the colour of mourning. In the West, red is synonymous with passion and lust, and so we see a lot of red cards, flowers and gifts for sale around St Valentine's Day. In China, it symbolizes long life and good luck, prosperity and good fortune, and is the colour traditionally worn by brides. It is the colour of the Chinese New Year, when people put money in red envelopes as gifts. Red is the colour of purity and love in India; when women marry, they colour the parting of their hair with red.

Green

Green is the colour of money in the USA. It is also the colour of nature and symbolizes the environment. In the East, green can symbolize fertility and new beginnings. It can also represent infidelity. In China, to wear a green hat is an expression that means your wife has been unfaithful to you. In Britain, it is the colour of jealousy; 'green-eyed' jealousy was first used by Shakespeare, in his play *The Merchant of Venice*. And, in Ireland, it is the colour of good luck. Green was the Prophet Muhammad's favourite colour and is the colour of Paradise. In South America, green is the colour of death.

Blue

In Japan, blue means fidelity. It is also one of the colours for good luck. In the West, blue is associated with sadness and feeling low, hence the phrase 'feeling blue'. But blue is the colour of Krishna in Hinduism and represents love and divine joy.

Yellow

Yellow is associated with pornography in China. It is also the colour of emperors. It is the colour of mourning and sadness in Egypt because of its close association with gold, which represents eternal life. In Japan, yellow is the colour of treachery, but it is also the colour of bravery. In Europe, it is the colour of cowardice, weakness and betrayal. Specifically, in Germany and France, it is the colour of jealousy.

Orange

In America, orange is the colour of the pumpkin and is symbolic of Halloween. In India, it is a sacred colour. For Buddhists, orange is the colour of spirituality and peace. In Japan, it is the colour of civilization and knowledge.

Pink

In China, where the colour was unknown until recently, the symbol for pink means 'foreign colour'. It is the colour of Tuesday in Thailand, and it denotes trust in Korea. It is the colour for little girls in English-speaking countries.

Purple

This is the colour of mourning for Thai widows and denotes sorrow. In the West, purple is the colour of royalty. The first purple was made from the mucus of sea snails. It took 12,000 snails to produce just over one gram. It was the Romans who made the colour a status symbol. Julius Caesar decreed that no one else was allowed to wear it except for himself. Elizabeth I wore purple to her coronation banquet in 1559, and, when she died in 1603, her coffin was draped in purple velvet.

Brown

In the West, brown is the colour of the earth and represents wholesomeness, fertility and nature. In India, brown is one of the many colours of mourning. In Japan, it can denote strength and durability.

Grey

In the West, grey is associated with old age, dullness and boredom. It can represent emotional sterility. It is the colour of ash and is the Christian symbol of the resurrection of the dead.

Dreams are often depicted in grey, and the colour can represent the unconscious.

The story of pink and blue

Often no one remembers the original reason for the meaning of a colour. It's slipped into folklore to become the way it's always been. A good example of this is blue for boys and pink for girls. This has been repeated so often that it has come to seem natural, as though we are biologically made to like these colours. But the assigning of gender symbolism to pink and blue is a relatively recent phenomenon. For centuries, in Europe and America, babies didn't wear colour at all. They wore white gowns. This was a matter of practicality. White could be cleaned more easily with bleach, and dresses were easier to deal with before a child was toilet trained. When colour did start to be worn by infants and children, at the beginning of the twentieth century, blue was considered to be the more delicate colour and therefore appropriate for girls, while pink was thought to be a stronger and bolder colour (pink being a faded red and red being a colour associated with masculinity) and so more suitable for boys.

By the end of the 1940s and the Second World War, this had switched around. Why, exactly, nobody really knows. There are stories that a US department store ran a campaign of pink for girls and blue for boys, and that it stuck – now that's marketing! It certainly made it easier for manufacturers to make everything in one of two colours, and, once everything for girls began to be made in pink and for boys in blue, it became natural to us.

There is nothing intrinsically masculine about blue or solely feminine about pink, however, and it shouldn't surprise us that these meanings are on the move again. The story of pink is far from over, as we will see later.

Colour in the everyday

———

But you don't always have to travel far to have meaningful colour experiences; they are all around you. I can be stopped in my tracks by a colourful weed growing from a crack in the pavement, a black bird against a clear blue sky, or the fresh, new colours of spring. To me, there is nothing more life affirming and uplifting than the many tones of green in the English countryside when the sun is shining. Coming from a sunburnt country (Australia), I still find it's one of life's miracles.

In this chapter, we have explored some of the many ways in which we perceive colour and seen that visual colour perception is very far from being a straightforward business. Men and women may see colour differently from each other. Some women may see more colours than the rest of us. Our neighbours may not see it quite the way that we do. And, for some of us, colour is a whole multi-sensory experience. We have looked at how we give colours names and wondered if naming them might actually help us to see them. And we have looked at some of colour's cultural meanings and seen how they vary across the world and shift in time.

But colour is not just a matter of visual perception, personal memories and symbolic significance. It has a powerful psychological impact. Colour has the ability to deeply affect how we feel and think, and to influence the way we behave. And this is the same the whole world over. Whatever cultural or personal meanings we ascribe to colour, when it comes to our inner lives, it has a universal impact. And, in the next chapter, we will look at how this happens. We will examine the psychology of each of the eleven colours and explore how they make us feel. We will see that every colour has positive and adverse attributes, and we will get closer to uncovering our unconscious responses to them. Whereas personal association and the cultural meaning of colour is largely conscious and conditioned, the psychology of colour is largely unconscious. It makes us feel something without our even knowing it.

CHAPTER 3

The relationship between colour and how we feel

How colour impacts on our psychological state

I have been itching to get on to this subject and to introduce you to concepts and evidence that show us just how fundamental colour is to our everyday existence. Colour is so much more than a visual conundrum solely to be studied in scientific laboratories. This is where the colour revolution starts to rev up, and where everything we have learnt about colour so far begins to slot into place. You are about to discover just how powerful a phenomenon colour really is and to learn how deep an impact it has on our every waking moment.

Remember what we read in Chapter 1, about colour being light, and light being energy? When that light strikes the eye, it is converted into electrical impulses, and those electrical impulses pass through the same part of our brain that processes our emotions. What scientific research has shown us is that every colour, and every tint, tone and shade of colour, has specific psychological effects. There is not one of those 16 million different colours that we can distinguish with our eyes that doesn't have a psychological impact, whether we realize this is happening or not. You have only to think of how we are affected by the colours of the natural world to see this in action:

how the sun's rays fill us with happiness and optimism, how the greens of a forest give us a feeling of peace and tranquillity, how a dark-grey sky makes us want to stay in bed under the covers. All these are our subconscious and unconscious responses to colour.

In the next pages, we will get to know the psychological traits of the eleven main colours that we established in Chapter 2 and discover the distinct and nuanced emotional effects of each spectral hue. We will see that the different emotional effects of a colour will depend on the context in which we see it, its saturation and how much of the colour is used. We don't see colour in isolation, however, and in the second half of the chapter we will look at some examples of how the psychological effects of colours can change when we begin to put colours together.

But there is one thing we need to do first, which will really help the psychological meanings of colours make sense to you, and that is to look at what we call the 'psychological primaries'. There are four psychological primary colours, each of which triggers specific, observable behaviours.

The psychological primaries

Red. Red affects us physically. Its primary action is to trigger physical responses. It raises the heart rate, causing our pulse rate noticeably to speed up, which can give the impression that time is passing faster than it really is. Red can activate the 'fight or flight' instinct: the physiological reaction that occurs in response to a threat or an attack.

Yellow. Yellow affects our emotions. Its primary action is to trigger emotional responses. It has an impact on the nervous system – a system that transmits signals to and from the brain to the rest of the body – making yellow the strongest colour in psychological terms.

Blue. Blue affects our intellect. Its primary action is to trigger mental responses.

Green. Green is the colour of balance and harmony. It sits between the physicality of red, the intellect of blue and the emotion of yellow. In essence, green is the balance between the mind, body and emotional self.

Whether a colour is stimulating or soothing to us depends on its chromatic intensity. If it is a deeply saturated colour, it is likely to be stimulating, and, if it has low saturation, it is likely to be soothing. Darker, more intensely saturated blues stimulate the mind, for example, while lighter, less saturated blues can soothe and calm the mind. A strong, dark red is physically exhilarating, but a soft, light red, i.e. pink, is physically soothing and comforting. The deeper the yellow the stronger will be its emotional effect. The deeper the green, the more we can feel its power to balance and rejuvenate us.

We will see these four psychological primaries in more detail when we look at the psychology of the eleven main colours shortly.

Quick psychology lesson

———

The mind is made up of:

| the conscious | the subconscious/ preconscious | the unconscious |

The father of psychoanalysis, Sigmund Freud, often used the metaphor of an iceberg to describe the mind. The tip of the iceberg represents the conscious mind – everything that we are aware of at any given moment, including memories, feelings, sensations and perceptions. Just beneath the surface of the water is the subconscious mind (sometimes called the preconscious). This is where the thoughts, feelings and memories that we are not immediately aware of – but that can easily be accessed – reside. Below this, submerged deep beneath the water, is the much larger bulk of the iceberg. This represents the unconscious mind. Here are all the beliefs, emotions, impulses, wishes, memories and instinctive thoughts whose access is beyond our deliberate control. For Freud, the most important part of the mind was the unconscious, the part beneath the surface, because it is the unconscious mind that drives our behaviour.

We will refer back to this concept in the next chapter, when we come to look at our favourite and our least favourite colours to try to uncover what meanings they hold for us and why.

conscious

subconscious/
preconscious

unconscious

The psychology of red

As we have seen, red affects us physically. Red has the longest wavelength and, even though it isn't the most visible colour, it has the appearance of being nearer than it actually is, attracting our focus – saying 'pay attention'. There's nothing shy or retiring about red, that's for sure! This makes red the ideal colour for traffic lights, stop signs, postboxes, warning signs. Anything you want to be noticed, and the same goes for human beings.

A series of psychological experiments carried out by researchers at the University of Rochester to examine how colours affect men's attitudes to women found that even a brief glimpse of red enhanced women's attractiveness to men. In the experiments, men who were shown pictures of women against a red background, or wearing red clothes, not only rated the women more attractive and sexually desirable than the same woman with no red in the picture, but – they were also more inclined to spend money on the woman in red and take her out on expensive dates!

Other studies have shown that when dating a woman dressed in red, men tend to ask them more intimate questions and show them more sexual interest. Men also offer more help to women in red, and male diners tend to tip waitresses wearing red lipstick or red clothes more generously.

Positive psychological traits of red

Some positive qualities of red are warmth, energy and excitement. It is the colour representing masculinity – the physical strength of energy such as stamina, strength, passion and, yes, lust. It relates to courage, rebellion and basic survival.

Adverse psychological traits of red

Some of red's adverse qualities are communicated through anger, annoyance, exhaustion and heated argument. Use too much red, or surround yourself with the wrong tone of red, and it can appear aggressive, confrontational and defiant. Due to its high level of physical energy, it can be tiring and overwhelming. Surround yourself with too much red and you could find it difficult to relax and unwind.

The many tones of red

There are many tones of red, from the warm (yellow-based) reds, such as watermelon, strawberry, russet and rust red, through to the cool (blue-based) reds, like raspberry, cherry, fire-engine and pillar-box red. Remember, red always triggers a physical response. The deeper and more intense the tone of red, the more physically stimulating it will be.

Red in action

Brands that project the qualities of red are outgoing, energetic – and more! Think of Coca-Cola. Red is the perfect colour choice for a drink that is all about the stamina, power and burst of energy it claims to provide.

Or let's take the Virgin Group. This brand is not shy about taking on the big, established firms at their own game. You could almost say it has a defiant, rebellious streak. This is a brand that gets away with being tongue-in-cheek. There is always a buzz of excitement about what they are up to next.

The psychology of pink

Positive psychological traits

Pink is the colour for an expression of a nurturing, caring and empathetic love.

As you can see, it is a very different kind of love from that which is associated with the physically stimulating red, but it is not the exclusive domain of little girls or women. Empathetic love is just as much for boys as it is for girls, and is just as easily expressed by men as it is by women. If cuddles were a colour, they would be pink.

Adverse psychological traits

On the opposing physical side, pink can come across as needy, weak or helpless. Surrounded by too much pink, men may feel emasculated.

In the early 1980s, a famous football coach at the University of Iowa decided to paint the visitors' locker rooms pink as a tactic to undermine psychologically the opposing team and stop them playing well by making them feel as if they were losing their physical strength. When, in 2005, Iowa rebuilt its Kinnick Stadium, it not only kept the pink lockers, but painted the urinals, sinks and showers in the visitors' locker room all pink too – to the outrage of many, who said it was in violation of the federal law that requires employers to treat its employees equally and schools to treat their students equally. It is, however, still pink to this day.

The many tones of pink

There are the warm baby pinks, blush pinks and nude pinks; and the cool pinks, rose pink, dusty pink, magenta and bubblegum . . . to name just a few.

The tone and intensity of pink can affect us differently. Soft, warm pinks, like baby pink, are physically soothing because of the low intensity of the colour. These tones suit the gentle energy of babies and young children. Strong, cool pinks, like magenta, are physically stimulating because of the high intensity of the colour. It could even appear to be quite feminist and feisty. I've had women tell me they see it as the grown-up version of pink, and it's increasing in popularity as women move away from masculine red and towards greater femininity, but without what many fear would be appearing 'girly' or 'weak' by wearing the softer pinks. I have noticed these intense pinks are frequently used by women who once used to wear a lot of red and often it's their first foray into pink.

Pink in action

Looking at the positive qualities of pink, it is easy to see why the softer, gentler tones would resonate with little girls. And marketers have been exploiting its emotional appeal. Over the years, the gendered use of this colour has become more overt, and has been applied to everything relating to little girls to the virtual exclusion of any other colour. The result of this is, in terms of colour psychology, predictable. When there is too much use of a colour, we begin to feel its adverse effects.

Could it be possible that little girls who love pink are connecting with its positive qualities, whereas the women who loathe it are feeling its adverse qualities?

In a series of experiments conducted in the 1970s, Alexander G. Schauss, now of the American Institute for Biosocial Research, examined the colour pink and its effect on mood and behaviour. Out of hundreds of different shades of pink, Dr Schauss selected one that gave the most consistent results in terms of lowering heart rate, blood pressure and pulse, and persuaded two military officers at the US Naval Correctional Center in Seattle to paint the walls and ceilings of an admission cell pink in exchange for giving the colour their names. Fifteen minutes' exposure to Baker-Miller Pink, as it came to be known, was found to be all that was needed to reduce aggression in the detainees. The effect was reported to last for as long as thirty minutes after leaving the pink room. 'Even if a person tries to be angry or aggressive in the presence of pink, he can't,' says Schauss. 'The heart muscles can't race fast enough. It's a tranquilizing color that saps your energy.'

There are pink prison cells in the UK, Germany, Austria and Poland. In Switzerland, 20 per cent of prisons and police stations have one pink cell. The colour is also known as P-618, Schauss Pink or Drunk Tank Pink.

MAGENTA

BUBBLEGUM

ROSE PINK

DUSTY PINK

BABY PINK

BAKER-MILLAR PINK

The psychology of yellow

The positive psychological traits of yellow

How do you feel when the sun is shining? Happy, spirits uplifted? Yellow is one of the psychological primaries and is related to the emotions and the nervous system. It has a relatively long wavelength and is emotionally stimulating, making us feel more confident, positive and optimistic. Yellow can boost our self-esteem.

The adverse psychological traits of yellow

The unfavourable effects are, of course, the exact opposite. The wrong tone of yellow, or too much, can lead to feelings of irritation, anxiety, nervousness and depression. At its very worst, yellow can provoke suicidal feelings.

The many tones of yellow

Looking at a few of the many tones of yellow, there's warm daffodil, buttermilk, magnolia, sunflower, saffron, mustard, ochre, and then cool lemon and fluorescent yellow. Many of my clients come to me thinking that yellow is a colour they just can't wear. But there is a yellow for everyone. It's just a matter of finding the right tone for *you* (we are going to explore this in detail later on). If I wear a beautiful, rich, saffron yellow, I will look drained and tired because it is the wrong tone of colour for me. But when I wear a clear, warm, sunshine yellow, I look and feel great.

Yellow in action

Yellow is the colour of sunshine, and sunshine brings happiness. Businesses whose ideal customers are children know that touches of yellow in their stores make for happy children – and when children are happy, parents are more likely to buy. Yellow has also come to symbolize the fast-food industry, particularly in combination with red. McDonald's is the most well-known example of this. The positive psychological messages in the combination of the tones of yellow and red they have chosen express happiness, excitement and fun. Children just know they are going to have a fantastic time from the moment they recognize that bright yellow *M*.

The other thing this combination of colours does is to get you energized and to move quickly, making it a perfect colour choice for a fast-food outlet. And, given customers don't linger in a McDonald's, the likelihood of experiencing the adverse effects of the colours is fairly minimal.

This is a different matter for the staff, however, who work long hours, taking in the heightened emotional effects of yellow all day – or night – long. This would definitely be a challenge, especially if no other colours are being used to provide an emotional balance in the staff break-room areas.

When using colour to influence behavioural change, it is important to think about the positive, supportive behaviours you want to create and to remember the possible adverse feelings the colour can give rise to. Using the right tone in the right proportion and in the right place is paramount if you want to create the effect you intended. It's no good thinking to cheer yourself up with lots of yellow because too much could have the exact opposite effect and just make the situation worse.

The psychology of orange

The positive psychological traits of orange

Orange is made up of red and yellow – which means it combines two of the psychological primaries, one that relates to the physical (red) and the other to the emotions (yellow). Yellow, as we have seen, positively communicates happiness, cheerfulness and optimism. Red's positive qualities, remember, express energy, strength and excitement. Together they produce a colour that is warm, friendly, energetic and fun, that expresses frivolity and playfulness, connecting us back to our inner child. Orange is mischievous in a good-natured way and is the colour that stimulates social interaction and friendly conversation. It is the colour that expresses abundance.

The adverse psychological qualities of orange

Too much, or surrounding yourself with the wrong tone, and orange can express the opposite: it can be seen as childish, frivolous, unrefined and cheap.

The many tones of orange

Some of the warm orange tones we know as peach, pumpkin, salmon, apricot and burnt orange; a cold orange is Persian orange.

The psychological qualities expressed will depend on the intensity of the colour. The feeling you experience when you look at an intense, bright orange will be different from the feeling you experience when looking at a softer orange. Because gentle orange tones like peach or apricot often contain a small amount of pink, they can also express romance in a sensual way.

Orange in action

What do you feel when you see a business using the colour orange? Here are two very different brands both using orange: the cheap and cheerful easyJet and the luxury-goods brand Hermès.

It is no surprise that a budget airline should have chosen a bright, lively orange. It plays into the positive feeling of sufficiency (everyone can afford to go on holiday with easyJet!) and communicates friendliness, helpfulness and approachability. However, if your experience of flying with easyJet doesn't correspond with the positive qualities of its brand colour, that message can get muddled and the adverse effects of orange will begin to be felt.

Orange is not usually a colour you would associate with a luxury brand. But, in the years following the Second World War, the only paperboard available from which Hermès could make their boxes was orange in colour. Not wanting to lose that brand awareness, Hermès has kept the colour ever since. This tone of orange also has a lot of black in it, which helps to communicate traditional values and a sense of quality.

The psychology of brown

The positive psychological traits of brown

Brown is the colour of the earth and wood, and is essentially a dark orange. We feel reassured and safe with brown. It is solid, dependable and grounded, like a strong reliable tree. It is serious like black, but in a softer way. Brown can be supportive, whereas black can come across as oppressive and unapproachable. Brown is also cosy and warm – think of wooden floors and logs in the fireplace.

The adverse psychological traits of brown

Brown can seem dull, lifeless and boring. It can be stubborn and unbending. It can lack humour and sophistication, and bring up feelings of heaviness. That same strong tree can also be viewed as unyielding and unaccommodating.

The many tones of brown

There are warm golden browns, beiges and tans, and richer, darker browns like chocolate, coffee, chestnut, and cool browns like taupes, wenge (which is a very black brown) and ash browns.

Brown in action

Hotels and traditional clubs can make good use of brown. The salon in the Hôtel de Vigny, in Paris, for example, uses brown to convey a feeling of Old World charm and understated refinement. This is accentuated through the use of natural materials like wood and leather. Here you know you can be comfortable and relaxed. You certainly won't be rushed in and out. You may find yourself spending longer here than you intended, easily settling in and making yourself at home.

BEIGE

TAN

CHOCOLATE

TAUPE

CHESTNUT

WENGE

The psychology of blue

The positive psychological traits of blue

Blue is the colour of the sky and the sea. Time and again, research shows blue to be the world's favourite colour – perhaps because we are surrounded by it. Remember that blue is a psychological primary colour and affects us mentally. Some of its positive mental attributes are logic and clarity of thought. Lighter tones of blue are associated with mental calm, serenity and reflection.

The adverse psychological traits of blue

Too much blue or surrounding yourself with the wrong tone, and you could find yourself feeling and coming across as aloof, cold and uncaring. Even though blue is the world's most favourite colour, used in the wrong context we can become wary of it.

When we see blue food, for example, we instinctively respond to it as poisonous and unsafe. Just thinking of blue strawberries or blue meat is enough to make your stomach turn! There is actually no such thing as blue food – and if you're about to say blueberries, take a closer look: they're purple. Blue is the colour most likely to suppress the appetite – when we are lost in thought, we are less likely to be focused on our stomachs.

We're now becoming more familiar with blue in sweets, but brands have had to do a lot of marketing around their use of the colour. They often try to make blue more popular with campaigns that encourage us to take a risk, a dare to try it.

NAVY

SKY BLUE

TEAL

ROYAL

MIDNIGHT

TURQUOISE

The many tones of blue

Warm blues include sky blue, periwinkle, teal blue, turquoise and cobalt blue. Cold blues include powder blue, duck egg, navy, royal blue and midnight blue.

The effect of blue on our minds will depend on the intensity of the tone. Light blue is mentally soothing, which makes it a great colour for sleeping and dreaming. The darker and more saturated the blue, the more mentally stimulating we will find it, helping us to focus and boosting our concentration. But, regardless of the intensity, blue will always evoke a mental reaction.

Turquoise is a blue that is uplifting and rejuvenating. The vibrancy of turquoise energizes and awakens the mind, so this is a hue to consider for the bathroom to wake up the mind in the morning. It's the tone that is likely to create unsettled sleep, however, so it is not a colour recommended for the bedroom.

Blue in action

A lot of businesses in the financial and banking industry use blue as their signature colour. Its positive psychological attributes include honesty and integrity, and help a brand to demonstrate approachability and expertise.

Blue is also the colour of choice for the technology industry. As the colour of communication, it is perfect for social media. Think of Facebook, Twitter and LinkedIn. The technology company IBM is actually known as the Big Blue.

Of course, if the brands don't uphold the positive values of the colour, the adverse traits are more likely to be felt and they could come across as cold, unfriendly and uncaring.

Blue is a common colour for uniforms. Companies with mid-to-dark tones of blue as their uniform colour are usually corporate-style businesses that want to communicate seriousness and authority while still being approachable. A dark-blue uniform will express a level of conservatism and tradition. A lighter tone of blue in a uniform expresses friendly communication and 'blue sky' creative thinking.

Blue is a good colour for school uniforms. Depending on the tone, blue can help students to focus and concentrate. It can also have a calming effect and open the mind to discussion and the sharing of ideas.

The psychology of green

The positive psychological traits of green

We are reassured by green on a very primitive level. Where there is green, we can find food and water – it equals life. Green falls in the middle of the colour spectrum, and the eye requires very little to no adjustment to be able to see it. It is, therefore, a very restful colour for us, and indicative of balance and harmony.

The adverse psychological traits of green

Too much green, or being surrounded by the wrong tone of green, can lead to feelings of stagnation and boredom. If green can represent new growth and life at one end of the spectrum, at the other it can communicate rot and decay.

The many tones of green

We can see more variations of green than any other colour, as was driven home to me when I took part in the colour-naming experiment with Dimitris Mylonas we looked at in Chapter 2. Among the many different tones of green, there are aqua, emerald, forest green, olive, khaki, sage, bottle green, mint, jade, moss, pea green, grass green, pine, chartreuse, seafoam green and pistachio.

The psychological effects you will experience will vary according to the tone and intensity of the colour. Aqua is uplifting and refreshing, whereas olive can feel heavy and lacking in life.

There is nothing relaxing or restful about lime green, however. It's what I call green's alter ego. The amount of yellow in lime green makes this hue full of life and energy. It can be invigorating and motivating, zesty and refreshing. You might find it a good colour for when you are lacking in inspiration.

Green in action

When walking into a business interior that uses the colour green, you start to relax. You will feel more restful, like you are back in nature.

You might have noticed that recently in the UK and throughout Europe, McDonald's has been changing some of its store colours to green. It's no longer about rushing in for a quick bite to eat. You can relax, get comfortable, even linger over a coffee. What's going on? Are they trying to target a more mature clientele, or to hold on to their original target audience, who have now grown up? Or perhaps they are after a slice of the Starbucks market? Maybe they just want to improve their 'green' credentials?

The psychology of purple

The positive psychological traits of purple

What we typically refer to as purple, but in the visible-light spectrum is known as 'violet', is a combination of the power, energy and strength of red with the integrity and truth of blue. It has the shortest wavelength of all the colours and is the last visible wavelength we see, therefore creating connections with a higher realm, the universe and beyond. It is the colour we link with spiritual awareness and reflection, which is why it is favoured by those following a spiritual vocation or for meditating. It is a colour for contemplation and the search for higher truth.

The adverse psychological traits of purple

Surround yourself with too much purple, or the wrong tone, and you could become too introspective and lose touch with reality. Using the wrong tone can communicate cheap and nasty faster than any other colour.

The many tones of purple

These include the warm – lilac, violet, aubergine – and the cool – lavender, mauve and royal purple.

Purple in action

Purple has been used by royalty, the wealthy and those in high office in the Church for centuries. Its elite status stems from the rarity and the cost of the dye. Julius Caesar decreed that he was the only one allowed to wear the colour purple. In the court of Henry VIII, the Earl of Surrey was accused of high treason for wearing the 'King's Colour'. Queen Elizabeth I forbade anyone apart from close members of the royal family to wear purple. Kings, queens and emperors, of course, believed they were God's representatives on earth and that they therefore had a special connection to a higher power – another reason, perhaps, why purple was such a significant colour for them.

It wasn't until 1856, when a student at the Royal College of Chemistry accidentally stumbled on a method of creating the colour synthetically while trying to make an anti-malaria medicine, that purple became more widely available. But it remained – and remains – a special colour. Emmeline Pethick-Lawrence, the editor of the Suffragette newspaper *Votes for Women*, wrote, 'Purple as everyone knows is the royal colour, it stands for the royal blood that flows in the veins of every suffragette, the instinct of freedom and dignity.' In Alice Walker's famous novel *The Color Purple*, Shug Avery tells Celie, 'I think it pisses God off if you walk by the colour purple in a field somewhere and don't notice it.'

Did you know that Cadbury has tried to patent the particular tone of purple they use for their confectionery to stop other chocolate companies from using the colour?

The psychology of grey

Pure grey is made up of black and white. It is neither one thing nor the other, neither yes nor no. Grey sits on the fence. It is indeterminate and uneventful. Given that it is virtually absent of colour, it draws no attention to itself. Grey is a colour that recedes, allowing more vibrant colours to take centre stage.

The positive psychological traits of grey

How often have you heard someone say, 'I just love grey days'?

Psychologically, pure grey doesn't have any positive qualities. Most of us feel low and want to hibernate when the sky is grey and there seems to be no colour anywhere.

But that doesn't mean that people don't respond positively towards it. As a colour that cloaks the personality, grey allows you to remain detached and to be left alone. People often use grey to quieten the emotional noise in their lives and can feel comforted by its presence. It can be used as a safety net and is easy to hide behind. In the home, surrounding yourself with grey is like cocooning yourself from the outside world, going into hibernation.

The adverse psychological traits of grey

Over time, however, what we initially find calming in grey can for some people become draining and tiring.

Being surrounded by too much grey can leave you feeling wrung out and depleted. I remember this happening to me on one particular occasion. I was meeting a friend at a café and running late; I rushed in out of breath. I felt myself instantly relaxing, looking at the walls of the café, which were grey. We both noted we felt ourselves unwinding and becoming more calm. However, that 'calming down' kept going and going, so that, by the time we left a couple of hours later, I no longer felt relaxed, but drained and tired. You might find that, if you sleep in a grey room, instead of waking refreshed you're reaching for a double espresso to get you going in the morning.

The many tones of grey

When it comes to grey, there are warm greys and cool greys.

By understanding the psychological effects of grey, you will be able to decide whether it's the right colour to use. You will also know that if you are feeling tired or drained, it could be the effect of the colour.

Grey in action

Could it be that the recent trend for all things grey has something to do with the rapid pace of change in the modern world? When things around us are confusing and we feel insecure, we do whatever we can to simplify the overwhelm. Perhaps it is no coincidence that, as the world has speeded up with new technology and globalization (not to mention increasing political uncertainty), we have found ourselves shifting to a simplified palette of white, grey and black – using grey as a means of protection, to feel safe and secure. One thing we can control is the emotional noise around us, and we do that on an unconscious level with the colours we choose to surround ourselves with.

I have found that talking about grey with people makes them more defensive about their use of it than any other colour – which makes sense: if we are unconsciously using grey to make ourselves feel safe and secure, the last thing we want is to give it up.

The psychology of white

The positive psychological traits of white

White is perfection. It is pure and unblemished, and gives a feeling of peace and quiet, simplicity and clarity. White can clear a cluttered mind and provide emotional safety.

The adverse psychological traits of white

But white can also be perceived as being cold, uncaring and sterile. It can be isolating and remote. It may help calm the noise, distraction and chaos of modern-day life, but it can do so to the point of shut-down. In the 1950s, all-white padded rooms and white strait-jackets in psychiatric hospitals were used as a way to lower emotional temperature.

Brilliant White

Did you know that the bestselling white paint is the hue we call Brilliant White? Brilliant White is a man-made colour that was developed after the end of the Second World War. It is the only colour that doesn't appear in the natural world, which is why our bodies find it difficult to calibrate and connect to it.

So why is it so popular? For me, this is a 'no-decision' colour choice, making it easy to use in large, seemingly utilitarian spaces like car parks, factories, stairwells or developments, where often little consideration is given to the way that people might feel. It is popular with architects, as it draws a space precisely and doesn't interfere with their design. I often have discussions with architects over their love of white to create clean, unblemished living spaces, and how this might impact on those who live there.

The many tones of white

These include the warm ivory white, pale cream, the cool oyster white, Brilliant White and pure white.

White in action

Hospitals are a good example of how we can experience a colour's psychological duality. On the one hand, the positive effects of white fit in with the aims of the hospital administration. White helps a space to appear hygienically clean, quiet and orderly. Patients, on the other hand, can experience the adverse effects, and be left feeling cold, isolated, afraid and even emotionally abandoned. Not the feelings conducive to a patient's mental or physical wellbeing or recovery. Often staff need to work doubly hard to make up for the cold, stark environment. You will have noticed that hospitals, care homes and schools are moving away from all-white environments as the detrimental effects on health and wellbeing have become more widely recognized.

The psychology of black

The positive psychological traits of black

Pure black is a colour that has many different traits (like red). While most women gravitate towards its glamour, elegance and sophistication, black can also convey substance and authority and add gravitas. Black absorbs all light and reflects nothing back. It can conjure an air of mystery, offer emotional safety by creating a protective barrier and even allow us to hide.

The adverse psychological traits of black

Pure black can also express the opposite of all its positive traits. On the downside, it can be seen as menacing and scary, cold, unapproachable and overly serious. Black can feel suffocating and give rise to feelings of heaviness and oppression.

Black in action

In 2018, black was worn by the attendees to the Golden Globe ceremony in Los Angeles – a ceremony as famous for the array of colourful gowns traditionally paraded down the red carpet as it is for the awards themselves. So why? As we will see in more detail in the next chapter, colour can express how we are feeling and thinking without our having to say a single word. It can communicate a complex sentiment all by itself. And this is what was happening at the Globes. Black can be glamorous and sophisticated, and it can be serious and determined. Worn in this context (serious), it conveyed and supported the sombre mood of the 'Me Too' and 'Time's Up' movements and expressed an authoritative, no-nonsense attitude: these men and women mean business and are not to be messed with.

Colour harmony

We have just explored the psychological traits of the eleven main colours, but, in fact, the meaning of a colour can completely change when it is combined with another colour. Take black and yellow, for example. As we just saw, some of the positive psychological qualities of black on its own are sophistication, elegance, glamour, as well as emotional safety and security. Yellow's positive psychological traits, you remember, include helping to foster a feeling of happiness. Yellow uplifts one's spirits, supports self-confidence and self-esteem; it is friendly and welcoming. Now let's look at what happens when we see these two colours together by taking an example found in nature.

When you see a black flying insect, you know that it is harmless. It might well be annoying, but you know it is not going to hurt you. It's a different story, however, when you see a flying insect that is coloured black and yellow. We instinctively know this isn't harmless. We can tell from its colouring that it's got a sting and is going to hurt us. Black and yellow in nature signals danger. It means 'stay away', and we do everything we can to avoid it.

And it means the same in our everyday lives too. Think about toxic or poison signs, high voltage signs and keep out signs. There is no need for us to redo what nature has already done so well. And it doesn't matter where we see this combination of colours, it sends the same signal. If you were to wear a black-and-yellow dress or to create a predominantly black-and-yellow colour scheme in a room, you'd evoke a feeling of sensory high alert. You'd be on the edge of your seat, muscles tense, ready to react, possibly even to run.

Working with colour is always a case of the whole being greater than the sum of its parts. We do not see colour in isolation, and the way colours work together is what creates our emotional response.

So how do we begin to figure out how colours relate to each other, which colours fit together well to create the positive behaviours we want to see – and which colours do not?

We are now about to enter the world of colour harmony – but not as you know it. I want you, for the moment, to set aside your personal colour preferences, which colours you like and which you don't, together with any preconceived ideas you might have about which colours go together. When people talk about colour harmony, they are usually referring to the relationship colours have with each other according to their placement on Newton's colour wheel – as we saw earlier in Chapter 1 – but there is so much more to colour harmony than that.

What I'm introducing to you here is called tonal colour harmony. It is one of the best-kept colour secrets out there and an absolute game changer. Unlike traditional colour harmony, tonal colour harmony posits that every colour in nature sits in one of four tonal groups. Colours from the same tonal group will always harmonize with each other. But when colours from one group sit alongside colours from another group, they will jar (one of my colour students said it was as if the colours don't like each other). This is the way that colours are arranged in nature. Think of a tree in all its autumn glory. All the many different reds, yellows and oranges exist in a tonal harmonious whole. There is nothing that looks out of place. Colours don't need to sit next to or opposite each other on a wheel to be harmonious.

The theory of tonal colour harmony is a principal tenet of the Wright Theory, which we looked at briefly earlier. Created about thirty years ago (but still little taught to professionals), the theory is the result of Wright's exploration of underlying patterns in the colour spectrum and their relationship to patterns of human behaviour. In the 1990s, scientists looked at the way in which Wright had organized colour into four tonal colour families and discovered that there are correlations between the colours within each group that are not shared by the colours from any other group, thereby establishing that tonal colour harmony is, in fact, an objective reality. In the next chapter, we will look much more closely at our patterns of behaviour and the ways in which we relate to these four groups of colours. But first let's look at each of the four groups and see for ourselves how every colour naturally harmonizes with each of the other colours in its tonal colour family.

Palette 1: Spring/Playful

You can instantly see that all the colours in this group are warm, clear, delicate and bright. They are yellow based, which is what gives them their warmth, and they contain no black, which is what gives them their clarity. These colours have an inherent bounce and vitality to them and all the lively, happy energy that we associate with springtime.

Among the many hundreds of colour names that fill this group are watermelon red, apricot, sky blue, aquamarine, lilac, cream, buttercup, sunshine yellow, apple green, coral, baby pink and camel.

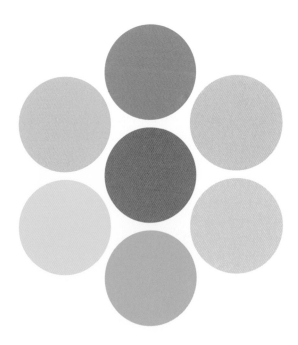

Palette 2: Summer/Serene

This is one of the two cool blue-based colour groups. With these colours, we have moved from the bright, playful energy of spring into the relaxed, soft mood of a hazy summer's afternoon. Each of the colours in this palette has a varying percentage of grey added to it, which is what gives them their distinctive cool, delicate and elegant tone. Think of antique roses, lavender and wisteria. The colours in this group are subtle and understated. They can be dark, but they are never heavy. Among the many colours we find here are rose pink, plum, sage, powder blue, lavender, mauve, taupe, oyster white and maroon.

Palette 3: Autumn/Earthy

Like the Spring/Playful palette, all the colours in this group are warm yellow based, but have more intensity. Each has a varying percentage of black added to it. This is what gives this group its rich, fiery depth. Remove the black from these colours and they would be just like the colours in the Spring palette. You can feel the earthiness of this palette, the grounding energy that we associate with autumn. The soft, muted tones of summer have been replaced by all the colours of harvest and autumnal leaves, rich rust reds, golden yellows, saffron, burnt oranges. These colours have a lovely weighty feel to them, whereas the colours in the Spring palette are so light you feel they might just float off. Colours in this palette range from the gentle and soft to the flamboyant and offbeat. They include olive, forest green, teal blue, aubergine, burnt orange, sunflower yellow, rust red, ivory white, chocolate brown and stone.

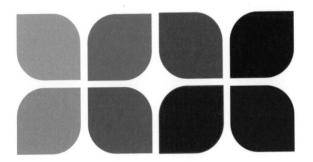

Palette 4: Winter/Minimalist

This is the second of the cool blue-based groups. The colours here are bold and dramatic. They are either intense or very icy – much like a minimal winter landscape. There is a sense of drama and power to these colours. There are no subtleties with this group at all. This is the only palette that contains pure white and pure black. Other colours here include magenta, lemon yellow, pillar-box red, pistachio, ice blue, pure grey, royal purple, shocking pink, charcoal, silver and midnight blue.

I believe, like Wright, that these four groups hold the key to universal colour harmony, that colours from the same group will always harmonize with each other, but that when you add in colours from another group they never will.

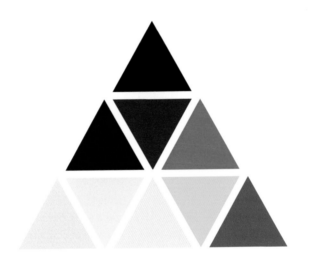

Another way to think about colour harmony is to think about musical harmony. It's believed that the famous jazz pianist Thelonious Monk once said, 'There are no wrong notes; only some are more right than others.' If you hear a note in the wrong key or out of place, you will notice it immediately. You might wince or give an inward shudder. And it's exactly the same when it comes to colour. If you use colour tones from a mix of different groups, you will instinctively sense that discord, even if your eyes don't register it. Put colours from the same group together, however, and there is that unmistakable feeling of harmony.

What you may not realize is that when you are out in the world, your subconscious is constantly calibrating everything around you to find out if it is in harmony or not. If it is, you will have a feeling of ease and comfort. But if your surroundings are jarring, you will feel the opposite. Your conscious mind may not articulate or recognize the problem, but your subconscious will certainly feel the disharmony inwardly and instinctively.

When it comes to putting a colour scheme together, the success or otherwise is down not to any individual colour, but to the tonal colour relationship the colours have with each other. If the colours don't harmonize with each other – or with the message or the context – it will create a discord. And, if you do that for a brand, it could mean a loss of sales; it could mean a loss of productivity in the workplace; and it could mean a loss of harmony in the home.

I'm not expecting you to get this straight away. Even the designers I teach find this new way of looking at colour challenging, but one of the things you can do is to pay attention to your own responses, as that's your subconscious telling you something. This is the start of becoming more mindful of true colour harmony; and the way to attend to it when putting your colour schemes together is to really tune in to your gut response to the colours you have chosen. If the colours tonally harmonize, you will feel comfortable and at ease. If they don't, you will feel uneasy or on edge. Notice where this feeling shows up in your body. With me, it shows up in my shoulders. When a colour scheme is off, my shoulders hunch up and tighten. But when the colour scheme is in harmony, my shoulders relax. I breathe out. It's like a sigh of relief.

Trust your gut. If a colour scheme doesn't feel right, it probably isn't.

In the next chapter we will look more closely at how to hone this sense and begin to put all that we have learnt into practice. I will guide you with tips, exercises and ideas to help you regain trust in your innate colour instincts and to banish any fears and hesitations you might have around how to use colour for ever. We will see how to wear colour to boost our confidence and happiness. We will look at creating colour schemes for the home that reflect and support all the personalities who live there. And we will learn how to surround ourselves with colour at work to help our concentration, ease our stress and to meet all the varied challenges of our working day.

When you understand that every colour, and colour combination, you choose can be used to create a positive emotional response, you will be able to create powerful and life-enhancing colour schemes in every aspect of your life – and you will be able to do it again and again. I have seen the way that colour can unlock happiness and joy – and now it's time for me to show you how to do this for yourself. So let's get going.

Colour and your personality

Colour and Your Personality

Welcome to Chapter 4. I'm so pleased to see you here. This is where we are going to take everything you have learnt about what colour is and how it works and use it to make positive changes in your life. I'm excited about taking you into this whole new world of possibility and self-discovery, and I know you're itching to get going, and we're nearly ready . . . There's just one more all-important step we need to take before you can put your newfound knowledge into practice. And that is to discover which of the four tonal colour palettes we learnt about in the last chapter is your natural colour palette, the one to which you instinctively belong.

Perhaps you have already noticed that you are intuitively drawn to certain colours? Maybe you liked one of the four palettes on the previous pages more than you liked the others? This is because each colour group reflects and expresses a certain type of personality: just as every tint, tone and shade of colour sits in one of the four groups, so does every one of us – and this is the case whether you are an individual, a brand, a shop, a hospital or a home. Like Jung, Itten and Wright, I look to the seasons as a way of explaining these four groups. Each season has a definitive colour palette and a marked personality that corresponds to the colour preferences and character traits of each group of people. There are also certain behaviours that align with the energy of each season. Think of how you feel in winter when the skies are grey and you want to hunker down and hibernate, or how awakened and alive you feel when the first bright flowers of spring appear.

Now you may be thinking that you have heard of seasonal colour palettes before. But this system is different. Many people come to me dissatisfied with the palettes they have been given when they have had 'their colours done'. Often they can't put their finger on what it is that's still missing. They might feel great in some colours yet not in others, and simply can't understand why. When I look at their palettes, however, I can clearly see that they include a mix of colours from all four tonal colour groups, so it's little wonder that something feels off. Remember earlier when I mentioned that sensation of disharmony with colours that don't feel right together: this is a perfect example of that happening. We know how out of place autumn leaves would look in a summer garden. I also think of these groups slightly differently: as Playful, Serene, Earthy and Minimalist in addition to Spring, Summer, Autumn and Winter. But, whichever way you choose to think of them, recognizing the four tonal families and how they relate to personality types is the first vital step towards using applied colour psychology successfully.

Over the next few pages you will find a set of questions designed to help you discover your authentic colour personality and design style. This is just a sample, of course, and there is a limit to how much personality analysis can be done from such a small selection of questions. I consult with my clients for several hours. I ask them about things that seem to have nothing to do with colour, like what kind of music they listen to, what they wanted to be when they grew up, where they like to go on holiday, what fabrics they like to wear, even whether or not they like to do the ironing . . . To begin with, they don't always see the connection. But, as we start to peel back the layers, taking them closer to who they really are, it all becomes clear. And I'm sure it will to you too.

One cautionary tale before we get going . . . This exercise is deceptively simple. It can be harder than we may think to get in touch with our true selves. Often we pick the answer we think we ought to pick, or that someone else would like us to pick. It's not at all unusual for us to select the type we'd like to be instead of the type we truly are. I dreaded this moment in my training, and was afraid of what the exercise might reveal about me. When the time came, I picked the colour palette that reflected the personality I wanted to be – and that was everything other than what I truly am. I was pretty stubborn and made life quite hard for my fellow students, who were learning how to carry out a colour consultation. When we got to the part of the training where we looked to see my physiological response to the tones of colours, I wouldn't even look in the mirror! But, deep down, I knew the truth. So I gave myself time. You may need to do the same. This is a journey of self-discovery, and the answers may not all come at once.

So find somewhere quiet to do this exercise, on your own away from anyone who might influence your answers. Don't overthink it. Trust your first instinctive response and pick the option that most resonates with you. This is about connecting to who you really are – not who you aspire to be, or who you think other people would like you to be. Don't worry about what anyone else thinks. This is a moment to be honest with yourself. And, when you are, it will feel like coming home!

Colour and Design Personality Quiz

1. **What is your favourite way to entertain guests for dinner?**
   A. Everyone seated at one long table, laden with plates of food from which they can help themselves; plenty of lively conversation
   B. An elegantly set table in a candle-lit dining room, full of Old World charm
   C. A picnic in the sunshine, with lots of fun and games
   D. Perfection – you might get a chef in or take guests to a Michelin-starred restaurant

2. **Which primary colour do you prefer?**
   A. Green
   B. Blue
   C. Yellow
   D. Red

3. **What is your favourite kind of social event?**
   A. Sitting round a fire with friends, talking deep into the night
   B. The ballet or a classical concert
   C. Musical theatre; something fun done on the spur of the moment
   D. An opening night or a premiere; a fashionable party

4. **What is your favourite type of jewellery?**
    A. Irregular style and shape, with an organic, natural look to it, made of copper, bronze, wood or amber
    B. Brushed silver or white gold and pearls; nothing heavy, flashy or ostentatious
    C. Light bright gold, sapphires, emeralds, opals; things that sparkle, have movement and catch the light
    D. Statement pieces; diamonds, rubies, black pearls, platinum

5. **Would you describe yourself as:**
    A. Sympathetic and interested in other people
    B. A quiet observer
    C. Outgoing and playful
    D. Self-assured, determined and driven

6. **How do you like to spend your time off?**
    A. Walking in nature or visiting an archaeological site
    B. Quietly, by a still lake
    C. On the beach, playing in the waves
    D. Lying poolside sipping cocktails

7. **What is most important to you in a home?**
    A. A cosy, homely feel
    B. Balance and proportion
    C. Plenty of natural light
    D. Simplicity and order

8. **What is your favourite type of film?**
   A. Historically based, biopic or nature documentary
   B. An old romantic black-and-white
   C. Comedy, preferably slapstick humour
   D. Film noir or arthouse

9. **You are called on to resolve a problem at work. What do you do?**
   A. Solicit other people's opinions and consider everyone else's view
   B. Remain cool, calm and diplomatic in your search for the perfect solution
   C. Enthusiastically motivate others to help solve the problem
   D. Gather all the facts; stay single-minded and focused on getting the right result

10. **What kind of music do you like to listen to?**
    A. Country and Western, folk, Indie
    B. Classical
    C. Pop music, musicals
    D. Opera, avant-garde jazz

11. **A friend is upset. What do you do?**
    A. You sympathize deeply, giving all your time and energy, and not leaving until you know they are going to be okay
    B. Quietly and calmly set about finding a way to help them
    C. You try to cheer them up
    D. You focus on fixing the problem

Now that you have answered each question, total up the corresponding letters to find out what personality type you are.

Mostly A: Autumn/Earthy

The archetypal Autumn/Earthy personality is warm and caring. Your intrinsic nature is one that is outwardly intensively expressive. You are interested in other people and in what makes them tick. You have an inquiring mind and a desire to understand. You feel happiest when you are in nature, whether that's pottering in the garden or walking in the woods. Relaxed and informal is your favourite way to entertain. You love to meet up with friends or have them round for a meal – just a small number, as you like to have close, deep conversations, sitting round a table piled high with plates of food or on comfy sofas by the fire.

The Autumn/Earthy type can also be quirky and flamboyant, with a rebellious side. You may appear to be bossy and dominating. Below the surface is a fire and, when pushed, it can roar.

In the home

A cosy and welcoming home is important to you. You like natural textures and materials, exposed brick, wooden floors, earthenware and copper pots. You might buy a house that you can renovate. You need to feel physically comfortable, so your furniture is solid, nothing light or flimsy. You like the comfort of a fireplace and an Aga or range cooker. You love books and trinkets and like to display your treasures on open shelves. You certainly don't do minimalist!

Fashion style

You like natural materials that have texture and pattern – raw silk, linen, tweed, brocade, damask, ethnic weaves, suede. Comfort is really important to you, so you care how clothes fit, even if that is loosely. And you'll do anything to get out of ironing. I have a good friend who before she buys anything does what she calls the 'scrunch test' – she scrunches the fabric in her hand, and if it doesn't crinkle, she buys it!

Jewellery

You like antique or old gold, semi-precious stones such as amber, jade and topaz, and the earthiness of copper, bronze and wood. Your pieces are substantial and solid. The shapes you are drawn to are organic and irregular.

The colour palette that goes with this personality is *Palette 3: Autumn/Earthy* (p. 104). These lively warm tones have a vibrancy and intensity to them. In keeping with the Earthy personality, they range from the warm and consoling to the flamboyant and quirky.

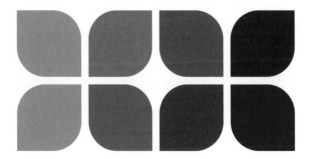

Mostly B: Summer/Serene

The archetypal Summer/Serene personality is dignified and composed. You are cool, calm and collected. Graceful under pressure, you are the calm in the middle of the storm. Your ideal night out would be something refined like a classical concert or the ballet. Your dinner parties are elegant affairs with everything matching and beautifully arranged. Your more extrovert friends might try to drag you up on to the dance floor, but you prefer to stand back and observe rather than be in the middle of the action.

Not someone who seeks the limelight, you are often taken for being shy. At times, you can be seen as cold, aloof and perhaps emotionally detached.

In the home

You like calm and order in your home. Your preference is for soft curves and graceful lines in your furniture and furnishings, nothing fussy or busy. You like fine craftsmanship and antiques made of woods like mahogany, satinwood and rosewood. You like the subtle sheen of satin paint, but nothing too high gloss or shiny. Proportion and balance are important to you and you will arrange things elegantly in pairs, like matching bedside tables with matching lamps.

Fashion style

Your style is one of understated elegance. You like graceful and soft, flowing lines. You are likely to have an acute sense of touch, so how something feels is very important to you. You prefer delicate, floating fabrics that have a slight sheen to them, like chiffon, cashmere and pure-silk jersey. Anything synthetic is likely to be uncomfortable, and you might even find that your skin turns red or itches.

Jewellery

Your preference is for silver or white gold that has a brushed or matt finish and gemstones such as tourmaline, pink sapphire or rose quartz. You also like classic pearls. The shape you are drawn to is oval.

The colour palette that goes with this personality is the cool *Palette 2: Summer/Serene* (p. 102). In accordance with the Serene personality, these are all subtle tones. Nothing loud or brash.

Mostly C: Spring/Playful

The archetypal Spring/Playful personality is outgoing and spontaneous, with a childlike sense of fun. The warm, lively energy of springtime is reflected in your eternally youthful nature. You are welcoming and friendly, enthusiastic and light-hearted. You can be mischievous and playful. You enjoy picnics, barbecues, anything outdoors with lots of people simply having fun. You love variety and spontaneity and doing something on the spur of the moment. You are great at motivating people in a cheerful, high-spirited way and like to make sure that everyone is okay.

While good at multi-tasking, you are likely to find focusing on just one thing challenging, and you can be seen as frivolous and superficial. Your emotions can be fragile. It is important to you to feel liked, and you worry about what other people think of you.

In the home

Natural daylight is essential to you. You like large windows so that light can flood in, and patio doors that open on to a garden or balcony – something to help you feel connected to the outdoors. You could find that you get SAD (Seasonal Affective Disorder) when you don't get enough natural light. You like furniture made from cane, wicker and light wood – nothing heavy. And you like gilded finishes and brass because of the way they reflect light. Favourite patterns for curtains and cushions are circles and dots – they have a fun and playful quality to them.

Fashion style

You like sheer, lightweight fabrics with a fresh feel that don't crinkle and can easily be ironed. Your preference is for delicate, light patterns of polka dots or small flowers, and floaty designs that have a lot of movement to them.

Jewellery

You like jewellery that is light and has movement. The gemstones you are attracted to are blue sapphire, opal, aquamarine and turquoise. The shapes you are drawn to are circles and dots, or small designs like flower buds and fine filigree.

The colour palette that goes with this personality is *Palette 1: Spring/ Playful* (p. 100). The clear, warm tones of this palette are full of life, lightness and energy, just like the Playful personality.

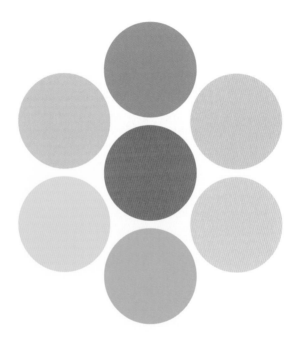

Mostly D: Winter/Minimalist

There is nothing compromising about this personality, which resembles a bold and icy winter landscape. The archetypal Winter/Minimalist is glamorous and sophisticated, with a pronounced sense of drama and a commanding presence. You are self-assured and confident in your taste and style. You are innovative and can be seen as avant-garde. Your dinner parties are meticulous affairs, with attention paid to every detail. The table setting will be stunning in its simplicity while also being an example of design excellence.

On one hand, you are efficient and focused, clear and concise. On the other hand, you can come across as unfriendly and indifferent. People can find you remote and unsentimental.

In the home

Your preference is for clean lines and clear surfaces in your home. You absolutely can't stand clutter. You love to have a single, striking centrepiece, like a chandelier, a sculpture or a large painting. You like shiny, glossy surfaces – such as glass and chrome – and sharp angles. You are likely to have a high-contrast colour scheme, for maximum impact. Your kitchen might look more like a laboratory than somewhere to cook meals, with spotless stainless-steel surfaces and everything hidden behind high-gloss doors, preferably in pure white.

Fashion style

Your style is polished and sophisticated. The cut of the garment is important to you. You like clean lines with no fuss or frills. You are likely to be attracted to solid colour, but you do like bold stripes and geometric prints. You look stunning in black and white. You'll settle for nothing but fabrics of the highest quality and you prefer those with a dramatic sheen such as heavy white satin or pure black silk.

Jewellery

Your preference is for a signature statement piece in shiny platinum or silver. Diamonds, rubies, onyx and jet are among your favourites. You like the precision of angular lines. The shape you are drawn to is the diamond.

The colour palette that goes with this personality is *Palette 4: Winter/Minimalist* (p. 106). Like the Minimalist personality, there are no subtleties with these colours, which are either icy or intense.

Primary and secondary personality types

It is very rare, however, to see someone who is purely one of these types. We are usually a combination of two or more. Carl Jung, you remember, hypothesized that we all contain something of each of the four groups, in proportions that vary with the individual, and that we are likely to connect with one colour energy in particular. Most of us have a primary personality type, with a secondary influence, in proportions that are unique to us. What I have found from the many consultations I have carried out is that our primary personality is the essence of ourselves – our true self – while our secondary personality is usually what we have been conditioned to become or what we believe is more acceptable – which is why so many of us live mostly out of our secondary personality. Our primary personality is what gives us our colour palette; our design style is influenced by a combination of primary and secondary. My primary personality type, for example, is the Spring/Playful palette, which means my natural colour palette contains all the clear, warm, light spring colours and I have a real sense of fun and mischievousness; and my secondary personality type is the Winter/Minimalist palette, which means that I can also be very focused and sometimes appear unapproachable.

If you found yourself also connecting with the palette that you scored second most highly in, you are likely to have connected to the two parts of your personality. This is great. It's exactly where you want to be. The beauty of applied colour psychology lies in its powerfully simple logic. Once you have an understanding of both your primary and secondary personality types, and know with which of the four colour palettes your primary personality is aligned, everything starts to slot into place with almost miraculous ease – as you are about to discover. Now you have done the *Colour and Design Personality Quiz*, you are ready to start using applied colour psychology. So let's get going!

PART 1

How to wear colour

How to reconnect with colour (and ourselves)

As we have seen, colour is our primary signalling system. It speaks to us in a language that we understand instinctively: the language of emotions. Whatever we put on makes us and other people feel something: every hair clip, piece of jewellery, hat or pair of shoes, from our underwear to our nail varnish. When we wear colour, we are saying something about what we feel and think, and it has a profound effect on how other people see us – whether we are conscious of this or not. A few years ago, when I was giving a talk on the power of colour and the impact it can have on our everyday lives, a man in the audience raised his hand. He said that colour had no effect on him and that he had no reaction to it. He was wearing black shoes, black trousers and a black shirt, arms folded throughout the entire talk. I asked him why he was dressed all in black. He said that it was not for any reason and it meant nothing to him. So I asked him whether he would wear a pink shirt, if I were to give him one. No way, he said; he wouldn't wear pink. When I asked him why not, especially as he had said that colour meant nothing to him, he replied that he wasn't going to wear a girls' colour – that would be ridiculous.

Well, I rest my case. Every one of us responds to colour; this gentleman just didn't realize that he was doing so. If colour didn't mean something, we wouldn't have fashions or trends or wear it for special occasions or events. We wouldn't bother with it at all.

And yet we do. One of the things that is so fascinating about us as a species is that we wear colour. We can change our outer layer to any colour we want, at any time. No other creature can go to a cupboard and take out a load of new feathers or pop into a shop and buy another skin to wear. We are the only species that can get a whole new layer, and that is actually pretty amazing. We can use colour like a magic wand, to boost how we feel, wherever we are, whatever we are doing – and no other creature does that!

However, we don't always realize the astonishing power colour has to nurture and support us and to make us feel good. If you have ever gone into a store having had your eye caught by a bright colour in the window, only to walk out ten minutes later with something in black, grey or white, you are not alone. There's no doubt that we love colour, but we can find it daunting. We are not sure what suits us; we worry that we'll get it wrong. Our instincts get drowned out by the endless macro and micro trends – by what I call colour noise. And there's a lot of it out there – on the catwalks, in magazines, shop windows, advertising and on social media. Some high-street fashion labels even bring out new trend colours every couple of weeks. We pick colours not for ourselves but to garner the approval of others, so they will like us, to be accepted or to blend in. And I know what that's like because I did it myself. Believe it or not, there was a time when I would dress all in black. And black rollnecks at that! My primary personality is very playful and fun. But I'm also tall and blonde, and, when I was in IT in my twenties, working as a project manager and business analyst, I worried about the way I came across. So I suppressed my playful side and put forward my secondary personality type, which is very focused and single-minded, results driven and self-contained. And I wore a lot of black. In part I was protecting myself, but I also wanted to be taken seriously. I pushed down my main personality type and let my secondary personality overshadow who I was. My colleagues called me 'the Ice Maiden' – which is not who I really am at all. Afraid to show my authentic self, I covered it up, right up to my neck, and disconnected from it altogether. I was very lost and low, unhappy in my job and in my personal life. And then one day I stopped and realized that, wow! I was so out of touch with myself that I didn't even know what my favourite colour was!

How to reignite your colour mojo

What's your favourite colour?

This may sound like a simple question. But there is much more to it than meets the eye. Looking at the colours we love – and, just as importantly, at the colours we dislike – is a valuable tool for understanding ourselves. Finding out about our favourite colour can reveal things about ourselves that we were not even aware of.

This is a perfect exercise for those of you who want to reignite your love of colour, or for those who are just plain curious about the power of colour to teach us about ourselves. Time and time again, I have seen clients light up with understanding when they do this exercise.

It comes with a word of caution, however. Remember, colour is emotion. Looking closely at the colours we love, or at those we dislike, can bring up deeply buried memories and, with them, powerful feelings. We may well have forgotten an event associated with a colour, for example, but we need only to see that colour for our emotions to be triggered.

Discovering what your favourite colour reveals about you

Step 1: Write down the name of your favourite colour. Being asked to pick a favourite colour might be like being asked to pick your favourite child! If you have more than one favourite colour, write them all down and then pick the one you like most from that list.

Step 2: Find the specific tone of the colour. If your favourite colour is blue, for example, duck egg or a pale sky blue or a deep navy or teal blue, find something in this specific tone. It might be a paint sample from a catalogue, a remnant of fabric, a feather, anything. Having the tone in front of you will help you to connect to it emotionally.

Step 3: So, once you've found the specific colour tone you like, you can begin to look at what it means to you. Remember what we have learnt about the three ways in which we relate to colour:

1. Personal colour association – a memory of an event you associate with the colour
2. Cultural or symbolic meaning – the meaning of the colour within your culture
3. Psychological meaning – how the colour makes you feel and behave

Tip: Your favourite colour could be a combination of two of these.

Once you have identified the way in which you relate to your favourite colour, write this down and describe why.

_____

_____

_____

_____

_____

_____

_____

_____

_____

_____

_____

_____

_____

_____

_____

_____

_____

_____

Favourite-colour exercise: troubleshooting

- If you don't have a favourite colour because you love all colours, pick a colour that is at the forefront of your mind right now.

- If you have more than one favourite colour, great: do this exercise with one and then you can do it with the others.

- If you're someone whose favourite colour keeps changing, pick the colour you like most at the moment.

My clients and students often say their favourite colour changes depending on how it's used. So it might help you to think about where you like to use your favourite colour. In your bedroom, perhaps, or in your office? Or perhaps think about when you like to wear your favourite colour. There may be special occasions when you like to wear it.

It wasn't until I was doing my colour studies, and I learnt about the positive and adverse aspects of colours, that I suddenly remembered that my favourite colour is orange (of course!) – the bright warm orange of a marigold. Orange is a combination of red and yellow. Yellow positively communicates fun, happiness, cheerfulness and optimism. Red's positive qualities express energy, stamina, strength and excitement. When you have orange, you have a combination of these qualities, a colour that is warm, friendly and playful. It makes me smile whenever I see it. It is a reminder of my essential fun-loving nature and connects me to the playful side of my personality. It's not a colour I wear very much, as it's a bit too high energy for me. But I love orange flowers. Just having orange poppies, tulips or marigolds in a vase at home brings me joy. I have a pair of orange shoes that I love. I look down and see fun on my feet!

What's your least favourite colour?

Interestingly, I have found that, while many people can really struggle to come up with a colour that they love, they often have no problem in identifying the colours that they don't like. So you might find this half of the exercise easier than the first half. On the other hand, the feelings that come up might be more difficult. Discovering the deep meaning of our colour preferences shows us what is happening on a subconscious level – a level of which we are not even aware. You may need to take your time here. If a colour brings up a memory that is difficult, allow yourself space in which to think about it. Give yourself permission to experience the feelings that come up. From my time with my clients, I've seen that uncovering what lies behind our least favourite colour can cut through years of therapy.

So, just as you did when choosing your favourite colour, now write down the colour you like least.

Discovering what your least favourite colour reveals about you

Step 1: Write down your least favourite colour.

Step 2: Find the specific tone of the colour.

Step 3: Once you've found the specific colour tone, you can begin to work out what it means to you.

Once upon a time, my least favourite colour was yellow. It didn't matter what tone of yellow it was, I just hated it. My fellow colour students actually called me Karen 'I hate yellow' Haller. But I didn't understand why I disliked it so much. Then one day, still during my colour training, it came to me in a flash. It must have been mulling around in my subconscious. I stopped the whole class with 'Oh my god, now I know why I don't like yellow. I've just realized!' I didn't wait for the teacher to say, 'Would you like to share?'; it all just came tumbling out. When I was a child, I had yellow furniture in my bedroom. A canary-yellow bed and headboard and a canary-yellow painted desk and shelves. And when I misbehaved, I was sent to my room. And since I was a child who was always pushing the boundaries, I was sent to my room quite a bit!

Even though I had long forgotten all this, the colour still made me feel bad. I attached feelings and memories to it. The colour was the trigger – and it felt the full force of my negative emotion. I made yellow wrong, but it wasn't the colour's fault! It seems so obvious to me now, but I had pushed those memories so far down that it took a long time for me to make the connection between the two things. This was my own colour-therapy session. Once I was conscious of why I didn't like yellow, I was able to detach my feelings from it. I went out that afternoon and saw a gorgeous yellow bikini in a shop window and went in and bought it. I love yellow now. It's my second favourite colour. I went from hate to love because I was able to disconnect the colour from the negative emotions I had unconsciously associated with it.

When I have clients who have a lot of resistance, or who can't work out why they don't like a particular colour, I encourage them to take their time. It took me nine months to figure out why I didn't like yellow. Don't worry if you're struggling to understand what lies behind your colour likes and dislikes. You might have that light-bulb moment in the shower tonight, or while walking the dog next week. But it will come, and, when it does, be prepared, because it will be emotionally charged.

How to put your best self forward

Find the colours that resonate with you

Now that you are reconnected to colour, it's time for it to work its magic – to boost your confidence, your self-esteem and your self-expression every time you put something on. And the first thing we need to do is find the tonal colours that resonate with you. This is the single most effective thing we can do to help us look and feel our best. When we are connected to the best part of ourselves, we can put our best self forward, no matter what the situation. So, select colours from the colour palette you identified with at the end of Chapter 3 and follow these steps to double-check that you have found your true colour personality and the colour tones that work best for you.

1. Ensure that you don't have any makeup on, so that you can easily see how your face reacts to the colour; this way, you will see the physiological changes, the slight shifts as they happen.

2. You'll want to be in front of a mirror with good light – natural light is best.
3. Hold the colour under your chin. What you are looking for is an overall glow to your face. It may be very strong or very subtle. If you are not sure if the colour works for you, put a colour that you know is not from your natural colour palette under your chin. You will see the colour drain from your face. Then put the other colour back against you.

- Does your face glow? If so, it's likely to be a good colour for you and you are likely to have identified your primary personality colour palette correctly. Do this with several colours to make sure.

- If you still look drained of colour, strained or tired, you might have identified the wrong tonal colour palette as your primary personality match, and may want to revisit your quiz results.

- Wearing the wrong tone of colour can create dark shadows on your face, leaving you looking washed out. Often we find ourselves applying lots of makeup to try to put back the glow that we have taken out by wearing colours that don't work for us. But when we dress in colours from our tonal colour family, we don't need much makeup at all. We will just naturally radiate.

A lot of women tell me that they will look around at what other people are wearing and try to apply that to themselves. They go out and buy an outfit they have seen look good on someone else or in a magazine, but when they get it home and put it on, they are disappointed. They don't understand why they don't look as good.

But, just because an outfit looks amazing on someone else, doesn't mean it will look amazing on us. That will depend on what colours make up the outfit and the tonal colour palette to which it belongs. Often, what we are really saying when we see someone wearing something fantastic is 'I want to feel as good as she looks.' But if the colours of that outfit are not in our tonal colour family, we won't be able to capture that feel-good look for ourselves. The way to do that is to dress in colours that belong to the natural colour palette that suits our personality type.

Remember that every colour has positive and adverse traits

If you are wearing a colour tone that does not resonate with your tonal colour palette, the adverse qualities of that colour will be expressed. Discord and disharmony will also be felt if you wear a mix of colour palettes – that is, a colour from your tonal colour family together with a colour that is not. And this will be particularly noticeable in the way that other people react to you.

It wasn't until I learnt about applied colour psychology and began to understand the different facets of my personality – the part that I suppressed in case I was thought childish, and the part that I put forward because I wanted to be taken seriously – that I could see what I had been doing when I had put on those black rollnecks and why my colleagues had reacted to me in the way that they had. Discovering my natural colour palette showed me the colours that suit me and support me, no matter what the occasion or situation, and those that don't – like black, as it happens. Black, I learnt then, is not a colour in my tonal colour family. It drains the colour from my face and leaves me looking tense and tired. So no wonder my colleagues had found me so frosty and unapproachable.

If I were to wear any colours that don't belong in my tonal family – like an olive green or a saffron yellow – I would look unwell, even though these are colours I love. In fact, in my first job out of school, whenever I wore an olive top that I had made (and was particularly proud of), my boss without fail would ask me if I were sick and wanted to go home. I would always look at her in bewilderment, thinking I was fine. Only later did I come to understand the effect the colour had on how I looked and why my boss responded to me in the way she did.

Wearing too much of a colour can also push it over from positive to adverse and affect the way in which other people see us. Sometimes less is more. Often we need only a splash of a colour to give us the support we need and to create the impression we want to give. Yellow might be a colour you love wearing, for example, but too much can be overstimulating and produce an effect you didn't intend. When all you need is a dash of the colour, you can bring in its positive emotional energy through your accessories – with a scarf, jewellery, a handbag, shoes or a belt. If you have to dress in a way that doesn't allow for your choice of colour, you can always wear the colour you need where it can't be seen: in your underwear.

Colour consciousness

Many of us just pull on our clothes without much thought. But knowing that every colour has its positive and adverse aspects allows us to be more mindful and consciously aware of our colour choices and what they are communicating. Whatever colour you wear will influence how you think and feel and how other people respond to you, so why not pick colours that support you in a positive way?

If you opened my wardrobe today, you would see blues, greens, yellows, pinks, purples, apricots, browns – the full spectrum of colours that I know suit me and that belong in my tonal colour family. I pick colours to wear according to how I'm feeling, what's suitable for the situation or occasion, and how I want to be perceived. I have left my black rollneck sweaters far behind. Now I know that, if I want to be taken seriously, there are colours that I can wear that communicate my natural authority without making me appear cold and unapproachable.

And I can be conscious of which parts of my personality to show at which times. We are all multi-faceted. Like everybody else, I have my lively, playful days and other days when I'm reflective and quiet. I have days when I need energizing and days when I need to stay focused. And for every mood and situation there are colours to match.

To choose the right colour for the right occasion, match the colours in your tonal colour family to the context in which you'll be wearing them. Use the following table to remind yourself of the positive and adverse aspects of a colour, and bear these aspects in mind when you are selecting which colour to wear for a particular situation. Consider the space that you will be in and who you are going to be interacting with in order to decide how much of the colour to wear, and where you might include it on your person.

Red

Some popular names
Fire-engine, rust, maroon, pillar-box, burgundy, vermillion, watermelon

Positive effects
Warmth, energy, stimulation, excitement, strength, physical courage

Adverse effects
Aggressive, defiant, demanding, dominant, impatient

When to wear
- When you want to get noticed – red appears nearer than it is so attracts our attention first
- If you want to come across as sassy/sexy
- To appear powerful and in control

Consider avoiding
When working with children as it can overstimulate

In healthcare

Meeting the parents

Pink

Some popular names
Rose, dusty pink, magenta, shell, pastel pink

Positive effects
Physically soothing, nurturing love, femininity – survival of the species, warm, supportive, compassionate and caring

Adverse effects
Emotional fragility and neediness, instability, emasculation, physical weakness, physically draining

When to wear
- Soft pinks: when working with babies and children
- To come across as caring and compassionate

Consider avoiding
Magenta and cold pinks: avoid wearing around children as they could come across as hard and cold

Yellow

Some popular names
Cream, daffodil, sunflower, saffron, mustard, acid yellow, lemon

Positive effects
Happiness, optimism, self-confidence, self-esteem

Adverse effects
Irrationality, anxiety, too much yellow can overstimulate the nervous system

When to wear
- When you need cheering up
- For a boost of self-confidence
- On a grey day to bring some happiness, to bring the sunshine with you

Consider avoiding
When you don't want to attract attention to yourself

In a serious situation where you might not be taken seriously

If you are already feeling anxious

Orange

Some popular names
Peach, apricot, burnt orange, Persian orange, terracotta, amber

Positive effects
Playful, fun, physical comfort such as warmth, food and shelter, sensuality, abundance

Adverse effects
Immaturity, deprivation, frustration, frivolity

When to wear
• Anything that is fun and playful – working or interacting with children
• It can lighten the mood, put a smile on people's faces
• To come across as approachable

Consider avoiding
When you want to be taken seriously – boardroom meeting, asking for a pay rise

Brown

Some popular names
Tan, camel, chocolate, taupe, clay, wenge, caramel, walnut, stone, beige

Positive effects
Warm, connects with nature, safe, reliable, serious, supportive

Adverse effects
Lack of humour, heaviness, lack of sophistication

When to wear
• When stability or grounding is needed
• To be taken seriously
• To be seen as being dependable/reliable

Consider avoiding
In a job where high energy is needed

Blue

Some popular names
Sky blue, duck egg, navy, turquoise, royal blue, ice blue, periwinkle, teal

Positive effects
Light blue: serenity, mentally calming
Dark blue: focus and concentration

Adverse effects
Cold, aloof, unfriendly

When to wear
• Light blue: when you want to appear approachable and friendly, to help soothe your mind
• Dark blue: to appear authoritative in knowledge
• Turquoise: when you want to be open to communication and idea sharing

Consider avoiding
Dark blue: avoid wearing during collaborative working and team-bonding sessions

Green

Some popular names
Khaki, olive, forest, bottle, sage, mint, apple, aquamarine, emerald

Positive effects
Balance, equilibrium, harmony, refreshing, rest, restorative, reassurance, peace

Adverse effects
Boredom, dull, stagnation –as in lifeless, decaying

When to wear
- Soft/dark greens help people feel at ease
- Lime green is full of energy – great if you are in sales (use as an accent colour)

Consider avoiding
Lime green, as people around you can end up feeling irritated

Avoid wearing lime green around children who need to focus and concentrate

Purple

Some popular names
Lavender, mauve, aubergine, royal purple, plum, lilac, violet, heather

Positive effects
Spiritual awareness and wisdom, composure

Adverse effects
Introversion, suppression, inferiority

Excessive use of purple can bring about too much introspection

When to wear
- When meditating or praying, helps promote deep contemplation
- It can help when wanting to focus on higher self
- Conveys luxury and quality

Consider avoiding
If wearing all the time may not be taken seriously

Pure Grey

Some popular names
This refers to pure grey (mix of black and white)

Positive effects
Pure grey is psychologically neutral

Adverse effects
Non-committal, lack of confidence, hibernation, energy draining

Fear of exposure, cloaking oneself, remaining hidden

When to wear
- When you want to hide and not be seen or draw attention to yourself
- When you want to remain impartial

Consider avoiding
When you need to be noticed, stand out

When engaging in collaborative teamwork

White

Black

Some popular names
Ivory, oyster, cream,
pure white, Brilliant
White

Positive effects
Hygiene, clarity,
purity, cleanliness,
simplicity,
sophistication,
efficiency

Adverse effects
Isolation, sterility,
coldness, barriers,
unfriendliness,
elitism

When to wear
- Wear for clarity of
  thought
- To have an
  uncluttered mind,
  and appear straight
  to the point

Consider avoiding
Can come across as
unapproachable,
cold, uncaring, elitist

Some popular names
Onyx, jet

Positive effects
Sophistication,
glamour, respect,
aspirational, security,
emotional safety,
gravitas, efficiency,
substance

Adverse effects
Oppressive, cold, heavy,
menacing, sinister,
draining, intimidating

When to wear
- When you don't want
  to be seen/stand
  out – waiting staff,
  backstage theatre
- To come across as
  the unquestioning
  authority – e.g.
  bouncers

Consider avoiding
- When working with
  children
- When trying to
  encourage open
  communication

What's in your wardrobe?

How often do you find yourself standing in front of your wardrobe thinking you have nothing to wear, even though it's bursting at the seams? And how often have you gone out shopping for clothes and come home with outfits in exactly the same colours that you already have? If you are anything like my clients when they first come to me, you may well find getting dressed in the morning fraught with anxiety. Why can't you find what you need when your wardrobe is so full? Why does the problem keep happening, even though you buy so many new clothes?

In the next few pages we will find out what's going on, and see how to build up your wardrobe to give you a colour for every situation and occasion, for however you want to communicate with other people and be perceived by them, and for gaining support for all your emotional needs.

What we are looking for when we stand in front of our wardrobes is the emotional energy of a colour: the colour that connects with how we are feeling, how we want to feel or how we want to interact with others. When we look in our wardrobes and think we have nothing to wear, what we are failing to find is the emotional energy that we need at that moment or want for a particular situation.

So let's take a look in your wardrobe and see what's going on.

What do you see when you open your wardrobe? Is there a range of different colours, or does one colour dominate? Use the spaces over the page to record what you find and to discover what characteristics these colours are linked to.

Colours in your wardrobe

Note down all the colours in your wardrobe.

If you find that you are consistently drawn to one colour in particular or to a range of similar hues, you may be seeking the psychological support this colour offers. Check in with the table on p. 154–7 to help you to find what you are looking for. Record here what the colours you like are linked to:

_____

_____

_____

_____

_____

_____

_____

_____

_____

_____

_____

_____

Colours missing from your wardrobe

Now note which colours are missing from your wardrobe.

_____

_____

_____

_____

_____

_____

_____

_____

_____

_____

_____

_____

_____

_____

_____

If you are avoiding a particular colour, this could be for an underlying psychological reason, a cultural reason or because of a personal association. It might even be a combination of reasons.

Record here what the colours you avoid are linked to:

_____

_____

_____

_____

_____

_____

_____

_____

_____

_____

_____

_____

_____

Colour combinations

Of course, as we discovered in Chapter 3, we never see colour in isolation and different colour combinations resonate with us differently. Do you have a favourite combination of colours that you like to wear or find yourself drawn to? You may be seeking the combination of qualities each of those colours provides. It is fascinating to look at what your colour combinations mean. You can experiment by adding a hint of another colour as an accessory and see how it makes you feel.

Record here what colour combinations resonate with you:

_____

_____

_____

_____

_____

_____

_____

_____

_____

_____

The essential aim is to have all the colours in your personal colour palette represented in your wardrobe, whether they are in your clothes, shoes, handbags, hats or accessories – anything that you put on. Having a full spectrum of colours in your wardrobe will support all your emotions, whether you need stimulus and excitement or peace and tranquillity.

Remember: All colours have their adverse psychological aspects too, so be careful not to bring out these characteristics. This is where you become your own guide. We all have our own responses to colour, and only you will know what is the right amount for you to wear on any given day. Some of us might be able to go head to toe in yellow, for example, and still feel all the positive attributes of the colour. Others might not be able to wear more than a splash of yellow before starting to feel its adverse qualities.

Wardrobe myth-busting 1: black is slimming

It is a myth that wearing black is slimming. It isn't. This is an example of one of those things that we have heard so often we've simply come to believe it. It's a cultural belief, but it isn't true. What happens when we wear black is that it conceals and camouflages the body. And the fact that we feel less visible to the outside world gives us the psychological belief that we are slimmer – but actually we look exactly the same.

Wardrobe myth-busting 2: black goes with everything

———

You've probably heard people say that everything goes with black. Well, this is a myth too. Black is often seen as a 'no colour' choice. When we are uncertain about what colours to put together, we often go head to toe in black – only to find ourselves wearing a bright colour to try to counteract how the black is making us feel.

What goes really well with black is pure white. That's why you see black and white together so often. They are the perfect pairing. Black is a cold colour, from Palette 4 (Winter/Minimalist), and looks great with all the hues in that group, so other cold colours work well with it – like magenta, which people mistakenly call hot pink. When you place a warm, yellow-based colour next to black – like a sunflower yellow or a watermelon red or a grass green – it will jar and create that discord that we talked about earlier. Look back at the Winter/Minimalist palette on p. 107 to see the type of colour tones that work well with black.

Someone who suits black will look striking in it – their faces will glow – but if black isn't in your tonal family, it can work against you, draining the colour from your face and making you look strained and tired. You might find yourself putting on a lot of makeup to compensate. I see a lot of women wrap a coloured scarf around their neck and shoulders to separate the black they are wearing from their faces. Perhaps instinctively they know it's not the right colour for them.

When you wear the colours that are your true colours, people's attention will go to your face. They will notice how well you look – and they will want to know what you've done that's different!

Workplace wardrobe:
getting over the Monday blues

———

In a recent survey, 22 per cent of women reported needing more confidence in the workplace, and 23 per cent said they needed a confidence boost on a Monday, compared with only 4 per cent on a Friday. The colour red topped the colour confidence poll, with its energizing 'get-up-and-go' attitude, and the colour grey was ranked the least motivational. Try using a colour from the list on the following pages for the area of your work life that you want to improve. This might be just what you need to get your week off to a flying start!

Giving yourself an instant colour boost

Red
motivation, energy, courage

Strong pink
vigour, tenacity, assertiveness

Soft pink
nurture, compassion, self-care

Yellow
optimism, self-confidence, happiness

Orange
playful, fun, joyous

Brown
supportive, grounding

Dark blue
focus, mental clarity, concentration

Turquoise
wakes up the mind, collaborative thought, openness

Light blue
creative thought ('blue sky' thinking!), tranquillity

Dark green
restorative, balance, reassurance

Light green
rejuvenating, refreshing

Purple
self-reflection, spiritual awareness

White
clarity, orderliness and simplicity

Colours to wear on a date

If you are going out on a date, think about how you want to feel and come across. Sassy? Demure? In control? More confident than you really are? Approachable? Fun? Remember that all colours say something and that whatever you are wearing, your date will react to it.

Research I helped to carry out in 2014 showed that 19 per cent of women would wear black on a date. You may feel glamorous and sophisticated in black, but, for many of us, black, as you now know, creates a barrier to hide behind. It might send a message that you are cool and aloof.

Magenta was another popular colour in the survey. Magenta represents the more feisty, feminist side of pink, and can send a message that you are an independent woman and not to be messed with.

Wearing grey might suggest that you are keeping yourself back and proceeding with caution. Perhaps you are testing the waters to see what sort of a person your date really is, without giving too much away yourself.

Wearing turquoise might suggest that you are a lively, chatty person who wants a good conversation.

Yellow can convey a sunny, cheerful nature.

How to create a colourful wardrobe – your personality in colour

Now that you have worked out your personality type and your tonal colour family, you are ready to make up your personal colour card and have some fun. I put the palettes I create for my clients on to a concertinaed card so that they can carry their colour personality around with them. In lieu of being able to do this for each and every one of you, here's a way to get started yourself. Collect samples of your colours – paint chips, cut-outs from magazines or pieces of fabric – whatever you can find. Pick the light and darker versions of each colour that belong to your colour family, so, for example, a mustard yellow and a sunflower yellow, a rust red and a nude pink, a chocolate brown and a tan. Think of it like a musical scale. Your personal colour card is your personality in colour – and you will find it useful for every part of your life, for the colours in your home and workplace as well as for the colours in your wardrobe. You will want to take it with you when you go shopping. It's easy to forget the colour we think we want when we are out looking for clothes and come back with something that was not quite what we were after.

I suggest going to a department store with lots of different ranges and brands. Once you are in the store, look for the colours in your colour group. If you put all the colours in your group together on the changing-room floor or hang them up, you will sense a certain vibration. There is an energy within each colour and when they tonally harmonize you can feel it. The best way to tell if you have found the colours in your particular colour group is to take a colour that you know *isn't* from your group and compare the two against your face. As we saw earlier, when you put on something that is in a colour from your tonal colour family, your face will light up.

When I go shopping, I pick colours along the scale and buy light, pastel versions and darker, saturated versions. I'm always on the lookout for colour tones that I know suit me. When they're 'in fashion', I'll buy several items because that colour might not come back again (let me know if you find something in the elusive watermelon red, because I'm always looking out for it).

Sometimes I shop for a specific colour that might be missing from my wardrobe, or for a colour I feel a particular need for at that moment. I can walk into the shop, do an initial 360-degree scan, spot that colour and make a beeline for it. Then I look at the style – the fabric, the cut, the pattern – and see if it belongs to my seasonal colour palette and suits my personality type. When all of these things are right, I know I will wear it and it's not going to stay stuck at the back of my wardrobe.

Re-creating your wardrobe can take time. There are budgeting constraints too. Don't get rid of everything immediately. There is a reason why you chose the clothes you bought, and you may have emotional attachments to them, so keep them until you are ready to let go. It can be daunting to recognize that you have been living out of a certain part of yourself and that the colours in your wardrobe haven't been serving you well when it comes to looking and feeling your best. It takes time to begin to live out the real expression of who you are. But you will find that the more new clothes you bring into your wardrobe, the more the colours of your old clothes will cease to resonate with you, and will, in fact, gradually seem out of place.

Dress yourself happy: colour challenge

Now you have regained trust in your colour instincts, it's time to experiment with the colours you've always wanted to wear but were too scared to try. When you understand your personal, individual relationship with colour, you can begin to have a lot of fun with your colour choices.

Use this diary to record the colours you wear on different days. Write down what you wear each day – e.g., Monday, red trousers, yellow top and orange shoes; Tuesday, coral skirt and jacket with soft-pink blouse and coral shoes – and note what happens. If you usually wear dark colours, notice if wearing lighter colours makes a difference to how you feel and to the way people interact with you. You may be surprised to see how wearing less saturated colours can lift your mood – and that people might interact with you in a much more positive way.

Monday			
Colours	How did you feel?	How did others interact with you?	The verdict?
Red trousers *Yellow top* *Orange shoes* *Orange handbag*	*It lifted my spirits, as I was feeling tired from a busy weekend* *Never worn these colours to work before so a bit apprehensive*	*They had big smiles, as they have never seen me out of my black and grey colours*	*My energy levels were upbeat and I didn't have my usual Monday 4 p.m. slump* *Will definitely wear these colours again*

Monday			
Colours	How did you feel?	How did others interact with you?	The verdict?

Tuesday			
Colours	How did you feel?	How did others interact with you?	The verdict?

Wednesday			
Colours	How did you feel?	How did others interact with you?	The verdict?

Thursday			
Colours	How did you feel?	How did others interact with you?	The verdict?

Friday

Colours	How did you feel?	How did others interact with you?	The verdict?

Saturday

Colours	How did you feel?	How did others interact with you?	The verdict?

Sunday			
Colours	How did you feel?	How did others interact with you?	The verdict?

PART 2

Colour in the home

There's no place like home

When it comes to our homes, there is nothing that has such a powerfully transformative effect as colour. Colour can turn where we live from just the place we go back to at the end of the day into a supportive, comfortable haven that expresses and reflects who we truly are. It communicates feeling, creates a mood, affects our energy, our appetites, our sleep, and has a profound effect on our emotional wellbeing and on the behaviours of everyone we live with.

So why aren't more of us using it? One recent survey I helped to carry out showed that 95 per cent of British people are too nervous to go all out with colour in the home. Another showed that 75 per cent of us are decorating not to please ourselves but to please other people: to increase the resale value of our homes, or to avoid offending the neighbours, or to please our family or friends. That means that many of us are going back to places devoid of the positive emotional support that colour can give us – and living in places we don't necessarily like in the hope that others will.

So let's change that straight away. You already have the tools you need. You know your colour personality and design style, you know your natural colour palette, and you know the positive and adverse traits of the eleven main colours. When we put these things together, we are ready to create positive emotional spaces that fit us as individuals and that support our needs, as we will see. Nothing creates a sense of belonging quite as much as colour does, and in the next few pages we are going to see how we can use it to connect us to ourselves and to turn our home into our sanctuary.

Before we get going, let's take a quick look at what can go wrong.

Five reasons why colour schemes fail (and what you need to know to create successful colour schemes every time)

Here are five reasons I have identified, gained from my experience of consulting for home owners and teaching designers, as to why colour schemes might fail.

Reason 1. There's a colour elephant in the room. Did you know that everyone has colour blocks? By which I mean we all have a resistance to a certain colour or colours. This is normal. Even if you work with colour, you will have a colour block. One interior designer I knew said that she would never let a client have the colour red. She didn't like it and so her clients couldn't have it. Never mind that it might have been exactly the colour that made her clients happy!

See the *Colour Detective Tool* over the page to really help blast through any colour blocks you might have.

Reason 2. We focus on creating a mood, rather than on behaviour. Colour will always create a mood, but what we are looking for is the impact it has on the way we behave.

The question you need to ask yourself is: what is the behaviour you want to see? We can't see a mood, but we can see behaviour. Your version of relaxed may not look like my version of relaxed or your friends'; for example, you may be able to relax only while watching television, but I prefer silence. We all have our own version of relaxed. When you know the behaviour you want to see, you can choose the colours that will support it.

Reason 3. We misunderstand the importance of context. As we saw in Chapter 3, the context in which a colour is used can change the way it is perceived. Remember that every colour has both positive and adverse psychological aspects, and that the aspect we are most likely to feel is determined in large part by the context in which we see it.

When using colour in the home, consider the context in which you want to use it. When you use a colour in the wrong context, you will create undesirable behaviours.

Red is a good example of how key context is to the way in which we understand a colour. Red in an adult's bedroom, for example, will have a completely different meaning to red in a child's bedroom.

Reason 4. Not tapping into the secret power of colour. You know by now that every tint, tone and shade of colour has an emotional impact. No matter what colours you are using and in what combinations, they are always going to create a response. When you are thinking about what colours to use, you want to create a positive emotional response. Think back to the psychological properties of each of the colours we looked at in Chapter 3 to help you to harness their emotional power.

Reason 5. Our colour schemes are not tonally harmonious. Remember what we learnt about tonal colour harmony in Chapter 3 and the unconscious way in which we are constantly calibrating the colours around us? When we use colours that don't tonally harmonize, we create schemes that make us feel anxious and uneasy.

One of the simplest ways of becoming more mindful of tonal colour harmony and how to use it when putting together your colour schemes is to tune in to your sensory response to the colours you have chosen, as we saw in Chapter 3. If the colours tonally harmonize, you will feel comfortable and at ease. But if they don't, you will feel the opposite.

The Colour Detective Tool (how to blast through colour blocks)

As we've just seen in Reason 1 on the previous page, we all have colour blocks. Here's a simple diagnostic tool that will help you to get to the bottom of any colour resistance you might have when you are decorating your home and help you to steer clear of that bucket of Brilliant White.

Step 1. Identify the colour or colours you have a fear of or block around. Take a note of the exact tone of colour, as this will be the key to your resistance. For example, you may love green, but just have a block around dark bottle green, or you may have a complete rejection of all yellows.

Step 2. Identify the origin of the fear or block. Look into the source of the fear or block. Is it:

Personal colour association. Our colour memories, as we have seen, can have a long-lasting effect on how we respond to colour. You might not like dark bottle green because it reminds you of your school uniform, and you didn't much like school.

Cultural or symbolic meaning. Cultural and symbolic associations can also lead to colour blocks. You might have a resistance to a certain tone of pink, for example, because of its association in the West with little girls and you fear appearing too 'girly'.

Psychological: how a colour makes you feel. You may have a block around yellow, as it makes you feel nervous and irritable. Or you may avoid red because it feels too overwhelming and you feel you lose your patience more quickly.

Tip: Your block or fear of a colour could be a combination of two reasons.

Step 3. Becoming mindful. Once you have identified where your resistance to a particular colour stems from, your fear will begin to lift. Often the realization that you have a resistance to a colour is all that is needed for the block to dissolve. This stage can't be rushed. You might have the realization and be able to let go of your resistance immediately. At other times, it could take days or weeks.

Breaking through our blocks can help us to reclaim colours that connect us to ourselves and support the behaviours we want to see. I often think of one of my clients who had a strong resistance to aqua. She flat out rejected it, though it was a colour that suited her spring-like personality. Working through the blocks in the way described above, we discovered the root of her dislike. She associated the colour with an aunt who had been unkind to her when she was a child. Her aunt had worn aqua clothes, aqua jewellery, coats and hats; her house was top to toe aqua, cushions, rugs, crockery, lampshades – I'm not surprised she had a problem with it. Recognizing where the block originated, however, helped my client to reclaim the colour for herself. Once she was conscious of the association, she could begin to disassociate herself from it. If she continued to resist the colours, her aunt would still own it. And she wanted to set the colour free – and enjoy the colour for herself. Her bathroom is now decorated in gorgeous tones of aqua. It gives her exactly the wake-up feeling that she wanted – and she gets it every day.

Tips for colours for different rooms:
Quick Reference Guide

When we understand that every colour can be used to create a positive emotional response, it becomes a powerful tool to affect our wellbeing; it has a transformative effect on how we feel, think and behave.

Red

Some popular names
Rust, russet, cherry, strawberry, maroon, watermelon, pillar-box, burgundy, fire-engine

Positive effects using the right tone for you
Feelings of physical energy, excitement, strength and courage

Adverse effects using the wrong tone or too much
Can feel overheated and aggressive, can lead to feelings of impatience or being emotionally overwhelmed

Ideal area in the home
Bedroom – passion (lust)
Dining room – can stimulate conversation (though too much red can turn a discussion from friendly to heated)

Best avoided
Any room that feels hot, like a kitchen, or receives full direct sunlight
Study, meditation room, as can overexcite

Pink

Some popular names
Pastel pink, nude, shell, rose, dusty pink, blush, fuchsia, magenta

Positive effects using the right tone for you
Feelings of maternal love
Nurturing, compassionate

Adverse effects using the wrong tone or too much
Can feel emotionally fragile, emasculating, physically draining

Ideal area in the home
Nursery – eases tension, soothing
Bedroom – can help with grief or loneliness

Best avoided
Avoid soft pink in a home gym, as it's physically soothing

Yellow

Orange

Some popular names
Daffodil, buttermilk, magnolia, saffron, lemon, sunflower, mustard, fluorescent yellow

Positive effects using the right tone for you
Feelings of happiness, optimism and confidence

Adverse effects using the wrong tone or too much
Can feel overstimulating, can lead to irritability and feelings of anxiousness

Ideal area in the home
Hallways – these are usually dark without much, if any, natural light

Breakfast areas – great if you wish to create a sunny, happy way to start the day

Brightens a dark space

Can create a sense of light, warmth and a friendly welcome

Best avoided
Bedroom – over time, a yellow bedroom is likely to mean waking up irritable and annoyed

Babies are very sensitive to colour frequencies, so avoid using cream, which also contains yellow

Spaces that already feel overheated

Some popular names
Terracotta, amber, peach, apricot, burnt orange, salmon, pumpkin, Persian orange

Positive effects using the right tone for you
Feelings of fun, playfulness and joy

Supports feelings of physical comfort, security and warmth

Stimulates appetite

Feelings of sensuality and passion

Adverse effects using the wrong tone or too much
Can feel too playful and over-stimulating

Too frivolous

Ideal area in the home
Kitchen, dining room – encourages socializing and stimulates appetite

Bedroom – look for soft peach and apricot tones

Best avoided
Study, meditation room – as orange can be playful and fun, you may find it difficult to concentrate

Brown

Some popular names
Tan, camel, ash brown, coffee, chestnut, chocolate, taupe, clay, wenge

Positive effects using the right tone for you
Feelings of warmth, cosiness, earthiness, safety and reliability, supportive

Adverse effects using the wrong tone or too much
Feelings of heaviness
Can make you feel stuck

Ideal area in the home
Rooms where stability and security are needed, for example, a study or living room

Best avoided
Darker end of brown in nurseries and infants' rooms. Brown can be too unyielding, without providing the restorative night's sleep they need

Blue

Some popular names
Sky blue, duck egg, periwinkle, navy, royal blue, turquoise, petrol, teal, powder blue, midnight blue

Positive effects using the right tone for you
Light blue creates feelings of calm and serenity
Can aid in reducing mental stress and relieving tension
Dark blue aids focus and concentration

Adverse effects using the wrong tone or too much
Can feel depressed, withdrawn, cold

Ideal area in the home
Bedroom – light blue helps to relax the body and prepares us for sleep
Study – light blue for creative, 'blue sky' thinking
Dark blue for focus and concentration
Bathrooms – turquoise for morning energizing and waking up the body and mind

Best avoided
Kitchen and dining areas – as blue can aid in suppressing the appetite
Spaces that already feel cold

Green

Some popular names
Apple, mint, forest, bottle, sage, jade, moss, pea green, pine, chartreuse, seafoam, pistachio, aqua, emerald, khaki, olive

Positive effects using the right tone for you
Creates feelings of harmony, peace, reassurance

Restorative, restful and tranquil

Lighter greens can be refreshing

Can help us to feel connected to nature

Adverse effects using the wrong tone or too much
Feelings of stagnation and lack of motivation

Ideal area in the home
Bedroom, study, home office, living room

A psychological primary colour – restorative and rejuvenating for the holistic whole

Best avoided
Using lime green in the bedroom – the yellow in this overstimulates the nervous system

Purple

Some popular names
Lilac, lavender, mauve, aubergine, royal purple, plum, violet, heather

Positive effects using the right tone for you
Luxury, quality, spiritual self-awareness, composure, wisdom

Adverse effects using the wrong tone or too much
Introversion, decadence

Can lead to a sense of inferiority

Ideal area in the home
Bedroom – for quiet, retrospective time

Meditation or prayer room – encourages deep contemplation

Best avoided
Kitchen and dining room – as the high amount of blue in this hue can affect the appetite (suppressing)

Pure Grey

Some popular names
This refers to pure grey (mix of black and white)

Positive effects using the right tone for you
Pure grey is psychologically neutral

Adverse effects using the wrong tone or too much
Can be draining; non-committal and sluggish

Fear of exposure, cloaking oneself, remaining hidden

Ideal area in the home
Works well as an accent or as a backdrop

Best avoided
A room that already feels cold, small or with little light, as it will make the space feel smaller and possibly claustrophobic

Nurseries, infants' and children's rooms. In a child's room, won't lead to restorative sleep but rather to feeling sluggish upon waking

Any areas where creativity is needed – you may feel sluggish, won't think clearly

Bedroom – likely to wake up tired

Black

Some popular names
Onyx, jet

Positive effects using the right tone for you
Sophistication, glamour, aspirational, protected

Adverse effects using the wrong tone or too much
Oppressive, cold, menacing, straining, intimidating

Ideal area in the home
Recommended for use only by those who have black in their tonal colour family

More supportive dark colours are dark browns, purples or blues

Best avoided
A room that already feels cold, small or with little light, as it will make the space feel smaller and possibly claustrophobic

White

Some popular names
Ivory, oyster, pale cream, pure
white, Brilliant White

**Positive effects using the right
tone for you**
Clarity, purity, cleanliness,
simplicity, sophistication, efficiency

**Adverse effects using the wrong
tone or too much**
Isolation, sterility, coldness,
unfriendliness, elitism

Ideal area in the home
Kitchen, bathroom (accent colour) –
creates feeling of cleanliness

Best avoided
If white makes you feel very cold,
then avoid using as the main colour
It can also feel sterile and isolating

Step-by-step guide to decorating and designing with your personal palette (and creating positive emotional spaces in every room, even if you are renting)

Step 1. Look at the behaviour you want to see in each room. If you are looking to create a relaxing space, ask yourself what relaxing means to you – it might mean being with your family having a sociable conversation or it might mean watching television on your own.

Step 2. Remember the importance of context. Any colour that is not used in the best context can bring out its adverse characteristics and lead to the wrong kind of behaviour. The *Quick Reference Guide* on pp. 186–91 will help you to work out if the colour you have chosen is the right colour for that room.

Step 3. Refer to your personal colour palette. Remember, your tonal colour group will always be determined by your primary personality type. Look back at the palettes on pp. 100–7 to remind yourself of the tonal colours that belong to your colour personality.

Step 4. Take into account your design style. Remember, your design style will be a combination of your primary and secondary personalities. Look back at pp. 100–7 and choose a selection of shapes, materials, surfaces, textures and finishes that belong both to your primary and to your secondary personality types.

Step 5. Think about colour balance and proportion. Remember that too much of one colour can bring out the wrong type of behaviour. Look at the *Quick Reference Guide* on pp. 186–91 to remind yourself of the positive and adverse traits of each colour.

The Personality Power Struggle (how to live in colour harmony)

Choosing colour in our homes can present us with a very different set of considerations from when we are choosing colour to wear, for the quite simple reason that we often share where we live with other people – our children, our partners, a group of friends . . . And they have their colour preferences too. When we share our lives with other people, it can be tricky to negotiate our way through one another's personal design styles, let alone colour choices. Often the person with the loudest voice wins – which means that everybody else might find themselves living with colours with which they are not well aligned and in a place where they can never feel quite at home.

So what do we do when we are caught in a personality colour struggle? How can we make sure that each of us gets our needs met and we can live in harmony together?

Your secret weapon: use the *Colour and Design Personality Quiz* (pp. 115–17) to identify everyone's primary and secondary personalities. (When we do the quiz with the people we live with, we can learn things about each other that we didn't know before.)

Use the *Colour Detective Tool* (pp. 183–4) to discover the reasons behind each of your colour preferences. There will be a reason for whatever colours you choose.

The *key decision*, the most important consideration for creating a harmonious colour scheme, is which tonal colour palette to go with.

The compromises. Once you have identified your personality types, you can begin to see where the overlaps are. Now you can begin to create a blend of styles and colours that will meet everybody's needs.

Let's take a fictitious couple, Jack and Melanie, to see how this can work. They have been arguing about how to decorate their new flat, and Melanie is just about to give in to what Jack wants, when she opens this book and discovers that there is a way through their power struggle after all. They take the *Colour and Design Personality Quiz* and discover that Jack is primarily a Winter/Minimalist personality with Spring/Playful as his secondary type.

Melanie's primary personality is Autumn/Earthy and her secondary is Winter/Minimalist, like Jack's primary. They look at where there is an overlap to help them decide on which tonal colour palette to go with, and agree to a Winter colour palette for their common shared spaces. They also agree that the study, where Melanie spends a lot of time on her own, can be decorated in her Autumn colours to give her the support she needs when she works. Melanie has come to realize that she prefers the lighter end of the Autumn colours, which leads them to choose the lighter end of the Winter palette for the spaces they share. This is also good news for Jack, as it supports his Spring personality's love of light.

So that's the key decision made and already they are beginning to feel better! Now it's on to finding ways to bring in the design elements that support the different aspects of their personalities. Knowing that Melanie is an Autumn, and that it is important for her interiors to have a natural, earthy feel, they look for ways to bring in texture and warmth in cushions, curtains, fabrics and accessories. Jack's secondary Spring personality needs supporting with plenty of light and delicate lines, fresh flowers and indoor plants. The Winter/ Minimalist personality that they share means that they both like clear surfaces with a minimum of clutter and that neither wants to see a lot of things on display. *Et voilà!* Understanding their colour personalities has helped them to create a harmonious colour scheme and design that reflects who they are and supports their individual needs. They have turned their home into a place that reflects them both and in which they can live harmoniously together.

Colours for the perfect romantic evening at home

Here are three tips to help you create the perfect romantic evening:

1. What does romance look like to you?

Romance can mean something different to each of us. What might be just the right amount of emotion for one person might be emotional overwhelm for the next. When preparing your room, remember that less can be more.

2. What is the colour of romance to you?

Pink is the colour that expresses qualities of love that are nurturing, caring and compassionate. Coral pinks and salmon pinks will show your sensual and more playful side.

Red conveys the masculine energy, expressing qualities such as vigour, stamina and strength. It also conveys exitement. In the context of romance, red expresses the passionate, lustful side.

Remember: no colour is seen in isolation, so think about the main colour you want to use and then a couple of accent colours. You might want to use your romance colour as an accent.

Caution: if you are thinking of using a red-and-black colour scheme, remember that in nature red and black indicates danger. Think redback spiders and red-belly black snakes. It can be seen as quite an aggressive colour combination ('Stay away or I may bite!'), so just be mindful if that really is the mood you want to create.

3. Bringing the colour in

There are simple, low-cost ways to bring the colour in. Look around your home. You may already have the things you need, such as candles, cushions, tableware, vases. It's a cliché, but nothing signals romance better than flowers and candles.

Considering the colour needs of children

Quite often the way in which we decorate our homes ignores the needs of the children who live there. We want our homes to have a certain feel and we often design the children's rooms in flow with the rest of the house – which means that our children do not always get the support they might need from the colours they are surrounded by. One mother I knew complained to me that she couldn't get her young son to wear any colour other than red. He had plenty of different colours in his wardrobe, but each morning he chose the same red clothes and screamed if she tried to put him into something different. I asked her what colour she had decorated his bedroom. It was beige, she said, like the rest of the house. Well, no wonder he wanted to wear red! Instinctively he was reaching for a physically stimulating colour. The beige was boring him. He needed more liveliness and excitement, and tried to provide it for himself in the clothes that he wore.

Look back at the steps for *The Personality Power Struggle* (pp. 194–6) and use them to help you to find the colours that will work for you and your child, and give each of you the support that you need.

Remember that using too much of a colour can bring out its adverse qualities and end up creating undesirable behaviours. I wouldn't advise painting a child's bedroom with any red, for example. It's likely to keep them excited, subconsciously giving them permission to be active, and you would likely struggle getting the child to go to sleep!

Decorating colour myth-busting:
paint dining rooms red to stimulate the appetite

———

Do you remember how in Chapter 2 we saw that red in Eastern cultures means good luck and prosperity? That is why you see a lot of red in restaurants, particularly in Chinese restaurants. It is to do with business. It is not to do with the appetite. Red is good luck for the owner of the restaurant and has nothing to do with encouraging us to eat. That's a Western myth.

If you are looking for a colour for a dining room, you could consider putting in accents of orange. Orange is a colour that helps to stimulate the appetite, and, as it's a fun, playful colour, it encourages socializing too.

Going beyond trends to create homes that reflect who we are

Marketers work hard to persuade us to rethink our decorating choices. Every few months paint companies release new hues, textile manufacturers produce new ranges, the shops are suddenly full of different colours, patterns, fabrics . . . What are we supposed to do, redecorate each season? It can be exhausting and confusing, even overwhelming, not to mention expensive! No wonder we lose our way and reach for the white paint.

I certainly don't believe in shoehorning in a colour just because it's on trend. But, now that you know what your tonal colour palette is, you will be able to find a match in the season's latest colours.

Let's say that midnight blue is the latest must-have colour. This is a colour that sits in the Winter/Minimalist palette. What you can do if you belong to one of the other three groups is to select a dark blue from your personal colour palette:

- a dark teal blue would do the trick for an Autumn/Earthy personality
- a cool navy for a Summer/Serene personality
- a cobalt blue for a Spring/Playful personality

When you use colours from your personal colour palette, you will create a home that looks like you, and not like someone else. When your home reflects you, you will be connected to it – and when you are connected to it, you will want to go home to it!

PART 3
Colour at work

Going beyond grey: colour in the workplace

The modern-day office is, increasingly, a far cry from the grey cubicles of yesteryear (thank goodness), the kind of uninspiring and unsupportive environment I sat in every day when I worked in IT and wore my black sweaters. When I look back, I'm not surprised that I was dressing in black right up to my neck. It was a way to protect myself, not just from that intense target-setting culture, but from the bleak, even ruthless environment in which I worked. I had just enough space above my desk to pin up a small map of the world and plot my way out.

We spend a lot of time at work and it goes without saying that it is vital to create workspaces that don't just help with productivity and motivation, but that care for the wellbeing, comfort and happiness of the people who use them. If employers want to get the best out of us, they need to look after us – which means creating interiors that inspire, encourage and support us through all the challenges of our working days. When our environments are supportive, we are more motivated, more creative, more consistently productive as well as happier and more fulfilled. If we like the environments we work in, we are likely to want to go to work, and enjoy our work. And isn't that a win–win situation?

The role that colour can play in creating effective and supportive workplaces is becoming increasingly obvious. More and more employers are beginning to understand that colour is just as vital to our health and wellbeing as natural light, the quality of the air, the ambient temperature, the furniture we sit on and proper food in the canteen. We need to feel nourished in the workplace – and colour is a form of nourishment. Companies have long recognized the power of colour to connect their brand to its market, and they spend billions making sure that their message is effective. Now it is time to pay attention to the power that colour has to evoke positive behaviours within the workplace and to help the people who are employed there thrive.

As we go through the rest of this section, I will show you how to harness the power of colour to support you in the kind of work you do, whatever kind of work that is. We will see that colour can be used to boost morale and motivation, increase concentration and focus, help with creativity and thought, enhance communication, sustain energy. You name it, there's a colour for it! And I'm going to introduce you to an exciting new tool that will show you how to bring colour into any and every working environment, to encourage wellbeing and support positive behaviours, whether you are a school, a hospital, a care home, a corporation of thousands, a tiny start-up, or just on your own in your office out in the garden shed.

When creating mindful interiors for workspaces, here are a few points to consider.

1. Context. What is the kind of environment in which people are carrying out their tasks? This could be anything from an open-planned office with 'fluid' working spaces, to a cramped back room full of boxes, a staff room or a breakout area.

2. Behaviour. Think about the ways you want people to behave in the workspace and the experiences they can have while working. Do you want them to have brain-storming conversations, or to be focused and quiet? What do these behaviours look like? How would you want those using the space to respond?

3. Colour harmony. Remember to use colours from the same tonal colour family. When the colours are tonally harmonious, you will create a harmonious colour scheme.

Think about the chromatic intensity. Remember that what determines whether a colour is stimulating or soothing is not its hue but its intensity. A strong, intense colour is likely to stimulate, and a colour with low saturation is likely to soothe.

Don't forget the proportions. If you've got the proportions of the colour right, it is likely to provide its positive qualities. If you have got the proportions wrong, the adverse aspects are likely to be brought out. Consider the placement. If the colour is right in your line of sight, it is likely to have a more forceful, direct and insistent impact than if it is behind you, or if you are sitting on it.

Only when you see how people behave will you know if your colour scheme is supportive and comfortable or aggravating and uncomfortable.

The Wellbeing Colour Chart

I often get asked, 'What is the one colour I can use to get my staff to work more effectively?' Well, of course, there is no one colour. It's just not that simple. If you have been following me up to now, you know that, when it comes to colour, there is no one-size-fits-all solution.

On the next page you will find an amazing tool to help you find the colours that are most likely to support the behaviours you want to see and the experiences you want to create at work. I have been using this framework for many years and have seen it work time and time again to help my clients create supportive, nurturing places for people to work effectively.

The Wellbeing Colour Chart incorporates everything you have learnt so far about how colour – and specifically combinations of colour – has an impact on how we think, feel and behave. Remember, you are always going to have colour in the workplace, even if it's just raw materials like wood, concrete or metal. So you might as well use it in a conscious and mindful way. This tool will show you how.

Remember, this is just a framework and the chart can be used in any situation.

The Wellbeing Colour Chart

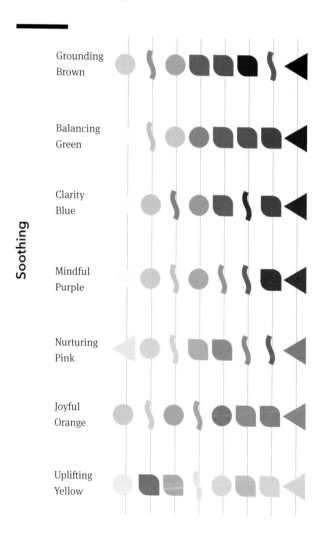

Soothing

Stimulating

Grounding Brown

Balancing Green

Clarity Blue

Mindful Purple

Nurturing Pink

Joyful Orange

Uplifting Yellow

Palette 1:
Spring/Playful

Palette 2:
Summer/Serene

Palette 3:
Autumn/Earthy

Palette 4:
Winter/Minimalist

Use this chart to help you find the colours and combinations of colours that best support you and create the outcome you want.

Consider how you want to feel on any given working day. This will change depending on how you feel when you wake up and on what you have planned at work: a board meeting, a difficult conversation with a colleague you've been avoiding, a presentation, maybe a deadline or just a busy day of 'to-do' tasks.

Remember that wearing colours that support you is a great way to put a bit of self-care into your working day.

Dressing for work

Red

Positive – This colour can give you that much-needed energy boost for the physically demanding day ahead of you.

Avoid bringing out the adverse traits of this colour – too much and you could appear aggressive, defiant and annoyed.

Pink

Positive – A great colour for when you need to show yourself some kindness and compassion and maybe give yourself a much-needed hug.

Avoid bringing out the adverse traits of this colour – too much and you could come across as weak, needy and insecure.

Yellow

Positive – Give yourself a burst of optimism, confidence and self-esteem and lift your spirits.

Avoid bringing out the adverse traits of this colour – too much and you could feel anxious or irritable.

Orange

Positive – Use this colour to bring a sense of fun and joy to your working day.

On the downside, too much orange in the workplace can be seen as frivolous and immature.

Brown

Positive – This is the colour for those times when our world is whirling and what we really need is to feel grounded and supported.

Be careful not to bring out the adverse traits of this colour. Brown can also be seen as humourless, too serious and lacking in sophistication.

Light Blue

Positive – A great colour for when you have a meeting that calls for open communication and you need to remain mentally calm.

Avoid bringing out the adverse traits of this colour – too much and you could appear cold and somewhat aloof.

Dark Blue

Positive – This colour can help you to remain focused on the task at hand, especially if it is detailed. It is a good colour to wear if you want others to know that you are knowledgeable, trustworthy and reliable.

Avoid bringing out the adverse traits of this colour – too much and you could appear cold, distant and unfriendly.

Green

Positive – Sometimes we just need to bring in feelings of balance and peace, especially when there is a lot going on in our lives.

Remember that too much green can lead to feelings of stagnation, boredom and lifelessness.

Purple

Positive – A great colour to help maintain personal spiritual awareness and focus or for when you need time to reflect.

Be careful to avoid bringing out the adverse traits of this colour – too much purple in the workplace and you could be seen as overly introspective and lost in your thoughts.

Grey

Positive – Grey is the colour for those days when all we want to do is come into work, get on with what we have to do and not be seen; it's a way of hiding oneself.

Avoid bringing out its adverse traits – a lack of confidence and indecisiveness.

White

Positive – When there is too much noise and emotional overwhelm, white can give us a sense of space and order.

Be careful to avoid the adverse traits of this colour. White can be cold and unfriendly and puts up barriers.

Black

Positive – Black can communicate unquestioned authority. It can also be used as a kind of shield – creating a sense of emotional safety.

Be careful to avoid bringing out its adverse characteristics – too much black and you could come across as cold, unapproachable or menacing.

Colour in your home office

More and more of us are working from home, at least some of the time. In fact, according to the Office of National Statistics, the number of people working from home in Britain has risen to its highest level since records began, with 4.2 million homeworkers in January–March 2014, or 13.9 per cent of all those in work. In the US it is estimated that some 30 million are working from home at least once a week.

That's a lot of us who need to find colours to help us meet the unique challenges of working on our own.

When you work at home, you have free rein to use whatever colours you need to help you get your work done. Which is wonderful. So this is about experimenting and seeing what colours support you and help you to work effectively. Ask yourself how you would like to feel and behave when you are working at home – and look at the colours that will give you those positive feelings and behaviours. By considering the colour of your chair or screen saver, curtains or cushions, the mug you drink out of and the clothes you wear, you can start to build a colour system that works for you personally. When you start behaving in the way that you want, you will know that you have got the colours right.

Here are some things to bear in mind when you are creating a workspace in your home:

- Choose a colour, or a combination of colours, that will support what you need in order to get your work done in a positive way.
- If you feel there are some colours you need only a hint of, you can always use them in accessories, stationery, plants or flowers. You can swap these out whenever you feel you need a change or if the type of task changes. If you need to be motivated to make those sales calls, choose a colour that will help you get into the right frame of mind. Swap the colour out when you put the phone down and want to concentrate on writing up your notes.
- Decide on the all-important placement of your colours – will they be in your line of sight, or behind you, or will you be sitting on them? This will make a huge impact on how you feel in the space.
- Consider the amount of each colour you are going to use – getting this right is key, otherwise you could end up feeling the adverse effects of a colour. For example, if you paint every wall in red because you need motivating, you could end up feeling overwhelmed, agitated and annoyed.

Your *N of 1 Colour Experiment* (to help you build your own personalized colour system)

An N of 1 is a clinical trial in which a single patient is the only case study. When it comes to colour in your home workplace, although not a clinical setting, you are your own N of 1 experiment. You are collecting your own data and carrying out your own research. Look at what your behaviours are like during the day. Are you sleepy in the morning, for example, or are you a get-up-and-go kind of person? Does your behaviour change at different times of the day or do you need to feel differently for different tasks? Use the worksheet and diary over the page to record how you feel and behave during the day and to map the colours over it. This will help you to create a personalized working environment that will nourish and support you whatever work you do.

Monday		
Task	**Colour**	**Feeling/Behaviour**
9am phone call	*red mug*	*motivated*
12pm accounts	*dark-blue desk mat*	*helped focus*
4pm flagging & tired	*orange flowers*	*made me feel uplifted when the work was tiring*

Monday		
Task	**Colour**	**Feeling/Behaviour**

Tuesday		
Task	Colour	Feeling/Behaviour

Wednesday		
Task	Colour	Feeling/Behaviour

Thursday		
Task	Colour	Feeling/Behaviour

Friday		
Task	Colour	Feeling/Behaviour

Saturday		
Task	Colour	Feeling/Behaviour

Sunday		
Task	Colour	Feeling/Behaviour

Preparing for a job interview or big presentation

———

Remember that colour can be used to boost our confidence, clarity of mind and presence, so when you are preparing for a job interview or big presentation:

1. Ask yourself:
   How are you feeling right now?
   How do you want to feel?
   How do you want others to interact with you?

2. Choose colours that will support how you want to feel – that might be authoritative, serious, open, calm, nurturing, kind, playful or fun. If it's not appropriate to wear the colours you would like, you can always wear them in your underwear, as we saw earlier.

3. Select the colours from your personal colour palette. We all want to look our best when we go for a job interview or have to stand up in front of an audience. One of the most effective ways to do this is by wearing colour tones that suit our personality. Wearing colours

that don't resonate with our authentic personality are likely to create a strain, both physically and emotionally, not just for us, but, crucially, for others. You will stand out when the tones of colour you wear are in harmony with your personality. You will look great, confident and comfortable, and everyone will sense this.

4. Consider the proportions of the colour you will be wearing. Be mindful that wearing a lot of one colour can bring out its adverse traits and create exactly the opposite effect to the one you intended, not just for yourself, but for other people too.

Colour tip: Before you accept the job, ask yourself what the colours of the workplace say about the company and what it might be like to work for them. Is it a place that is likely to be supportive and meet your needs? Or a place where you will be ignored and feel unsupported?

Colourful plants in the workplace

One of the quickest and easiest ways to bring colour into the workplace is with colourful plants. Plants are great stress busters. They have been proven to reduce sick days, increase productivity and enhance creativity. Back in my corporate days, I would often find myself bringing in a colourful pot plant or vase of flowers to put on my desk and lift my spirits.

Yellow is a welcoming colour – a cheery smile – so yellow plants in a reception are a great way to make staff and visitors feel welcome

Think of: golden pothos, 'Yellow Goddess' amaryllis

Purple is great for quiet contemplation and reflection, so purple in a breakout area can help to create that 'moment of calm' ahead of an important meeting or interview

Think of: oxalis, violas, African violet

Red is the colour equivalent of an espresso shot – it will give you an instant energy boost to help meet a deadline or give you the stamina to make a difficult client call

Think of: geraniums, tulips, Christmas cactus

Orange elicits fun and playfulness, so using orange in a brain-storming session can help stimulate creativity and joy

Think of: kalanchoe, marigolds, poppies

Soft pink is a nurturing, compassionate colour, perfect for consoling a colleague who has missed a promotion or had a rough day

Think of: begonias, phalaenopsis orchid, 'Triostar' calathea, Wandering Jew

Strong pink is feisty at heart – the perfect colour for challenging the status quo or showing you're no pushover

Think of: pink quill plant (*Tillandsia cyanea*)

White elicits clarity, so white plants on a desk can help to declutter the mind so that you can think clearly

Think of: peace lily, jasmine

PART 4
Colour in relationships

Colour IS relationship

When writing this book I looked up the word 'relationship' in the dictionary and this is what it said:

relationship, *n.*

The way in which two or more people or things are connected, or the state of being connected.

The way in which two or more people or groups regard and behave towards each other.

Well, isn't that pretty much exactly what colour is and does? Colour connects us to each other and to ourselves. It tells other people what we think and feel, and it influences the way we behave. It really is that simple. It is a way of connecting and communicating – a non-verbal conduit, a channel through which meaning flows. When we see colour, we see in an instant how someone is feeling and we know how to respond to them, even if what they are saying is 'Don't talk to me.' Colour is integral to our relationships and plays a role in every interaction we have, with whoever that may be. Including ourselves.

So let's see how we can take our colour consciousness up a notch to help improve those interactions. In the rest of this chapter, we will recap and tweak our skills. We will look more closely at the power colour has to deepen and strengthen our relationship with ourselves and bring harmony and happiness to our relationships with others. I will show you how to keep on track on your colour journey and remind you how to use colour for self-care and wellbeing – for, let's not forget, when we look after ourselves we are infinitely better able to look after others.

How colour can enhance our relationships with ourselves (and others)

Nothing is better for our relationships than knowing who we really are – which is why it is so important that we find our colour personality. When we are in colours that align with our personalities, our interactions with other people can be harmonious. Whenever we are in colours that don't fit with who we are, we create tension and unease, not just for ourselves, but for everyone around us. Living in the true expression of ourselves, we are being honest about who we are, and when we are more honest with ourselves, we can be more honest and open with other people.

A few years ago, a woman called me to arrange a personal colour consultation. She was concerned that she was shy and quiet and felt unequal and uncertain in her relationship, worried that her husband found her dull. She asked me if I could show her how to dress in bright colours to help her to come out of her shell and 'liven her up' a bit. I explained that the consultation would reveal what it would reveal, and that I wasn't going to put her in bright colours just because she wanted me to. That would go against everything I do, which is to explore with my client their authentic personality and not to use colour to manipulate them into something they are not.

In fact, the consultation showed her to be a Summer/Serene personality type, a quiet observer and deep thinker who suited low chromatic hues and who shone in her palette's lovely lavenders and pinky greys. The vibrant shades she thought she should wear would have had the opposite effect to the one she wanted. Far from livening her up, they would have drained the colour from her face, making her look strained and tired. And, far from bringing her closer to her husband, they would likely have taken her further away. Putting her in colours that didn't align with who she was would not just have created a disharmony we all would have felt – her husband included – it would have been forcing her into a false personality. And then who would her husband think he had married?

I have had clients who have left their relationships, having grown in confidence in who they are and then seen that the relationship was not right for them. And I have had clients who have grown closer to their partners, able to use what they have learnt about themselves to help them to communicate better. I can't predict what will happen in your relationship – but I can guarantee that when you know your true colour personality, you will be able to approach it with truth and honesty, from your authentic self, and that is the best way to be in our relationships, isn't it?

Colour personality recap

The exercises in this book have all been designed to help you to get closer to who you are, to open up your mind and help you to bring out what you know about yourself deep down. When we think about our favourite colour or answer the questions in the *Colour and Design Personality Quiz*, we can begin to connect to a place that is very deep within us. This is a way of thinking about ourselves that can take us further than we are used to going. And it can be a very healing, helping way for us to relate to ourselves. As we peel back the layers of false self, we can begin to mend the rift between who we think we ought to be and who we really are.

My consultations last several hours, and I take my clients through processes that allow them to come to their realizations themselves. I have seen people connect deeply with themselves, even those who have done a lot of personal development and belief work. I love to watch the way their faces change as their false selves slowly drop away and who they truly are begins to shine through. Of course, I would like to do a personal colour consultation for each and every one of you, and be there with you as you go through this process. But, since I can't, here are some pointers to take you further on your colour journey and to keep you on track.

Take a break

We can get overwhelmed by taking in lots of new information. My design-industry professional students all have wobbles. It's normal. We need time to let what we are learning sink in. So go and make yourself a cup of tea, go for a walk, or, if you're reading this book in bed, go to sleep. Do something that for you is the natural way for your mind to take a break. I like to potter in the garden, or, when I'm back visiting Australia, to go for a swim in the ocean. These are all new concepts, and you will need time to process them.

Review your primary personality type

I remember a woman in one of my workshops. As we went through the four different palettes and personalities, she kept selecting the Minimalist style and the Minimalist colours, the magentas, pillarbox reds and lemon yellows, and went for an austere, hard-lined, almost futuristic look in her designs. I noticed, however, that she didn't speak in the direct, clear, focused kind of way that is typical of the Winter/Minimalist type. In fact, she had a flowery and elaborate way of talking, full of embellishments, moving her hands around in a way that is much more like the Autumn/Earthy type – which made me wonder . . .

It didn't surprise me when, halfway through the afternoon, she took me to one side and said, 'Actually, this is my husband's style – even sitting here when this is meant to be about me I've been talking about my husband!' She had been with him for so long that she had taken on his style and design aesthetic, and forgotten about her own.

In my consultations and workshops I often have to remind people that they are there for themselves and steer them away from answering out of their work or home personalities. It can be tricky to let go of all the social expectations of us, especially if you're a woman – you're a mum, a wife, a daughter, a carer . . . So, redo the *Colour and Design Personality Quiz* whenever you feel the need to check and refresh your connection with yourself.

Or try this double-check. I have my clients put together a collection of pictures to bring into workshops – anything they resonate with and that they feel expresses them: pictures of activities like rock climbing or bicycling; landscapes or gardens, wild woods or flowers; photographs of friends or people they admire; clothes, cars, boats, sheds, castles . . . Most of the time my clients will be who they are in the pictures they have brought along, though they may have picked a personality they thought they ought to display or one they aspired to take on. You too will be able to see the consistency between the pictures that express you and the type of personality you have picked for yourself.

Refresh your connection with your colour palette

Did you get your primary and secondary types the right way round when you did the *Colour and Design Personality Quiz*? Remember, your colour palette belongs to your primary personality, and your design style will be a mixture of your primary and secondary personalities.

At the very beginning of my consultations, I hold up all four colour palettes for my clients so that they can see for themselves with which palette they instinctively connect. I note this down and then put them away. Then I go through the conversation part of the consultation, in which I'm asking questions and I'm getting to know them. This is the all-important psychological part of the process.

Then, when I'm sure of their two most 'clear' personality types, they go and sit in a chair. Once in the chair, in front of a full-length mirror in good natural daylight, I put sets of colours underneath their chin. Together we look at the effects they have on them. We look for physiological change, for example:

- skin colour (lost colour, tired, drained of colour, colour in their cheeks, a glow)
- eyes (brighter, more sparkly, duller)
- body (relaxed, tight)
- breath (breathing easily, tightening up)

And for the psychological effect, I ask them what they feel about each of the colours as we go through them.

When we have concluded together which is their primary personality, I pull out all the swatches from that tonal group. All the colours in this group will suit them, but now we are looking for the colours within the group that suit them best and personalize them more. When you do this for yourself, look for colours

- to help you to be taken seriously
- to express your softer side
- to relax you
- that make you stand out

And look for your signature colour, or 'Wow' colour, because that's what everyone says when they see you in it.

Remember that we are changing and developing all the time and our relationship with colour changes too. We evolve with our colours and our colour choices. Often the colours we say we don't like are the parts of ourselves that we don't want to express. But when you know your colour palette, the colour will be waiting for you when you are ready. One of my clients traces her personal development in her relationship with the colour pink. She connects it to herself as a person and as a woman. 'I'm maturing into pink,' she said to me recently, which I think is a lovely phrase and sums up our relationship with pink so well: it can take a certain amount of maturity to re-embrace it.

Give yourself permission to feel what comes up and go at your own pace

You will have many 'Ah ha' moments on your journey. You may find yourself saying, 'Gosh, I never knew that about myself!' Or 'Gosh, I always knew I was like that!' Being true to ourselves is a courageous thing to do and a lot of stuff can come up. So give these moments space and go at the pace that feels right to you. We all have our own individual way of moving on. Some of my clients are bursting to make changes and throw out all their old clothes and redecorate straight away. Others like to take their time, hold on to their old clothes until they are ready, or keep them as reminders, to measure their development and see how far they have travelled on the road to their true selves.

Using colour to balance our emotional lives

When we know our colour personality, we can choose to surround ourselves with the colours that meet our needs and support us in how we want to feel, whatever we are going through, be it illness, divorce or grief. So it is important to remember all the other things we have learnt about colour and how it affects us: that colours can be stimulating or soothing, that they have positive and adverse effects, and that the context and the proportions and the places in which they are used determine whether it is the positive or the adverse effect that we will feel.

And balance is key to this.

A friend of mine was going through a difficult divorce, and, wanting to feel safe, reassured and at peace, she picked a soft, warm green tone to decorate her new home. She used it in almost every room and, to begin with at least, received the positive psychological support from the colour she had been looking for. But, after a while, I noticed that she became lethargic. She no longer went out so much, and I could see that she had lost her drive and energy. The positive traits of the green she had chosen had turned to adverse. She had begun to stagnate.

I had been wondering if this would happen to her, and, if so, how long it would take. That's a lot of green, I had said to myself when she'd started to decorate. It's possible she might not have felt the adverse traits of the colour. We are all different and we all respond differently after all. But there is usually a tipping point when you've used too much of one colour, and all the positive traits you had been searching for are lost – or become the opposite. It's a bit like when, instead of taking one or two chocolates out of a family-sized box, you eat the whole lot in one go and then feel sick. When you use too much of one colour, you can have too much of the feeling it gives you. You can be emotionally overwhelmed. And, just as when we feel sick from eating too much chocolate we say we are never going to eat it again, so what we typically do when we have used too much colour is swing the other way and go all white or all grey to shut out the emotional intensity that has become too much for us.

What I've noticed is how often we swing between the two extremes. After a while of white or grey, we start to crave colour and the emotional support it gives us – and reach for the paint pot again. And, after a while of living with intense saturation of colour, it becomes too much and we go back to white. It's like yo-yo dieting, except with colour. When people go on a diet, they deprive themselves of food, of nourishment. When they end or break the diet, they often swing the other way and overeat. They swing right past the balanced diet.

Balance is important to us. Remember Hippocrates in Chapter 1, the father of modern medicine, and his theory of the humours. In Hippocratic medicine, all four humours had to be balanced, according to temperament. When the humours are in balance, we are healthy and happy. But when they are out of whack, we succumb to depression, illness and disease. Living at either end of the spectrum is detrimental to us. What we need to thrive is balance, and we can find it in our colour schemes by remembering proportion and placement. When we have the right amount of the colour, in the right amount of saturation, in the right place, the emotional pendulum stops swinging. When we are emotionally centred, we are better able to face the challenges that life can throw at us. Good emotional balance allows us to prosper and be happy.

Sources and further reading

Always Kalanchoë, 'Find your "happy colour"!', May 2018, *Always Kalanchoë*: https://www.kalanchoe.nl/en/inspiration/find-your-happy-colour/

Bell, Bethan, 'Actresses and arsonists: women who won the vote', *BBC News*, February 2017: https://www.bbc.co.uk/news/uk-england-42635771

Berlin, Brent, and Paul Kay, *The Basic Color Terms: Their Universality and Evolution*, University of California Press, 1969 (CSLI Publications, new edition, 1999)

Best, Janet, *Colour Design: Theories and Applications*, Woodhead Publishing Ltd, 2012. Chapter 20, Colour in Interior Design, written by Karen Haller

Bhatia, Aatish, 'The Crayola-fication of the world: how we gave colors names, and it messed with our brains (Part I)', *empiricalzeal.com*, June 2012: http://www.empiricalzeal.com/2012/06/05/the-crayola-fication-of-the-world-how-we-gave-colors-names-and-it-messed-with-our-brains-part-i/

Cherry, Kendra, 'What is the unconscious? Freud's conceptualization of the unconscious', *Verywellmind.com*, May 2016: https://www.verywellmind.co m/what-is-the-unconscious-2796004

Eckstut, Arielle, and Joann Eckstut, *The Secret Language of Color: Science, Nature, History, Culture, Beauty of Red, Orange, Yellow, Green, Blue, & Violet*, Black Dog & Leventhal, 2013

Gilliam, James E., and David Unruh, 'The effects of Baker-Miller Pink on biological, physical and cognitive behaviour', *Journal of Orthomolecular Medicine*, 1988, Vol. 3 (4)

Goethe, Johann Wolfgang von, *Theory of Colours*, John Murray, 1810 (trans. Charles Lock Eastlake, 1840)

Grahl, Bernd, 'How do Namibian Himbas see colour?', 2 September 2016: https://www.gondwana-collection.com/blog/how-do-namibian-himbas-see-colour/

Guéguen, N., 'Color and women hitchhikers' attractiveness: gentlemen drivers prefer red', *Color Research and Application*, 2012, Vol. 37, pp. 76–8

—, and C. Jacob, 'Lipstick and tipping behavior: when red lipstick enhances waitresses' tips', *International Journal of Hospitality Management*, 2012, Vol. 31, pp. 1,333–5

Haller, Karen, www.karenhaller.co.uk

—, 'Make yourself at home with colour', May 2016, *Karenhaller.co.uk*: http://karenhaller.co.uk/blog/make-yourself-at-home-with-colour/

—, 'UK homes "unadventurous" as 75 per cent admit to obsessing over impressing their neighbours', August 2013, *Karenhaller.co.uk*: http://karenhaller.co.uk/blog/uk-homes-unadventurous-as-75-admit-to-obsessing-over-impressing-their-neighbours/

Hammond, Claudia, 'Do colours really warp our behaviour?', *BBC News*, April 2015: http://www.bbc.com/future/story/20150402-do-colours-really-change-our-mood

Itten, Johannes, *The Art of Color*, John Wiley, 1973 (second edition)

Kandinsky, Wassily, *Concerning the Spiritual in Art (Über das Geistige in der Kunst)*, 1911 (Dover Publications, translated and with an introduction by M. T. H. Sadler, revised edition, 2012)

Lindsay, Kenneth, and Peter Vergo, *Kandinsky: Complete Writings on Art*, Da Capo Press, 1994

Melina, Remy, 'Why is the color purple associated with royalty?', June 2011, *Livescience.com*: https://www.livescience.com/33324-purple-royal-color.html

Mylonas, Dimitris, www.colornaming.com/ and https://www.researchgate.net/profile/Dimitris_Mylonas

Niesta-Kayser, D., A. J. Elliot, and R. Feltman, 'Red and romantic behavior in men viewing women', *European Journal of Social Psychology*, 2010, Vol. 40, pp. 901–8

Parker, Steve, *Colour and Vision: Through the Eyes of Nature*, The Natural History Museum, 2016

Walker, Alice, *The Color Purple*, 1982 (Weidenfeld & Nicolson, 2017 edition)

Walker, Morton, *The Power of Color*, Avery Publishing Group, 1991

The Wizard of Oz, Metro-Goldwyn-Mayer, 1939, screenplay by Noel Langley, Florence Ryerson and Edgar Allan Woolf

Wolchover, Natalie, 'Why is pink for girls and blue for boys?', August 2012, *Livescience.com*: https://www.livescience.com/22037-pink-girls-blue-boys.html

Wright, Angela, *Colour & Imaging Institute Report*, University of Derby, 2003/4: http://www.colour-affects.co.uk/research

—, *The Beginner's Guide to Colour Psychology*, Kyle Cathie, 1995

Acknowledgements

Writing this book has been a wonderful, colourful ride. It's been an all-consuming adventure, and, never being one to shy away from a challenge, I've loved and cherished every moment of it – and would do it all again in a heartbeat!

To Itten and Kandinsky: thank you for your visionary thinking. It was because of you both that I first began my own colour quest. Thank you to all my colour teachers – I know I drove you crazy with my endless questions – and especially to the teacher who had the biggest impact on me: Angela Wright. Angela was the teacher who was truly able to answer all my questions and guide me through the world of applied colour psychology with such depth and clarity.

Tamsin, who'd have thought all those years ago, when I mentioned wanting to create a revolution in how we embraced and used colour, that this is where it would take me? Thank you for your endless gentle nudges in getting me to face my biggest fear: public speaking. I'll never forget you ringing me up to tell me you had booked me to speak live on radio. You have helped to give me the courage to speak up and speak out about colour, even though for many years it did feel like I was just talking into the wind.

A huge thank you to the team at Penguin Life for entrusting me with the job of writing this book. I can still vividly remember the moment (it was on a Tuesday afternoon and I was about to finish for the day) that I noticed an email with the subject line 'Hello from Penguin'. Hyperventilating, I thought to myself, 'It can't be . . . ' and I wasn't even halfway through reading before I was dialling the number . . . 'Hi Aimée, it's Karen. I wanted to ring you straight away as I was worried your email might self-combust!'

Hearing Aimée's laughter was the beginning of a great relationship, and it was when we met and she showed me her vision for the book's structure that I was blown away: I pulled out the outline I'd written five months earlier and we realized we had both spotted the same opportunity to bring a book like this into the world. That was the beginning of my amazing journey with my editor Aimée Longos. I'd often heard that the relationship with your editor will be an important one, and, Aimée, thank you so much for all your support, especially when I rang you three quarters of the way through the writing to say, 'I think I'm having a bit of a wobble.' Your guidance was a godsend. Thank you for giving me the freedom to write the book I've been bursting to write for years. And to the incredibly amazing Anna Vaux for your patience in digging deep and then deeper still to get out of me more than I realized I had to say, and turning my words, thoughts and stories into a joyful, colour-filled, page-turning journey. Thank you too to Donna Poppy and Ellie Smith: your diligence and persistence in ensuring the manuscript was at its best cannot go unrecognized.

I've been fortunate enough to travel while writing this book and want to thank the wonderful people who let me squirrel myself away in their homes to write. On Australia's Gold Coast, where my mama would come into the room with cups of tea and plates of food. In Sydney, with Juliette Ridge, writing in between ocean swims. In Switzerland, with my cousin Eveline Haller, staying with her in the Swiss Alps (yodelling was optional). Soo Hammond and John Whittle on their cool glamping farm in Wales, Tamsin Fox-Davies and Alan Grattan in Kent, Yvonne Gurney in a little English village (with no shops or pubs – unheard of!), and Alison and Andy Struthers in London complete with the fabulous company of Millie the black Labrador.

Thank you to all my clients, students and industry peers for challenging me in so many ways both personally and professionally, and for enabling me to carry out my research, and put all I've learnt into practice. Thank you, Dimitris Mylonas, for being so generous with your time and knowledge.

Thank you to my dear friends for their unwavering support and all-round cheerleading skills, always bolstering me up and encouraging me to keep going over the years – Andrea Grimmond, Ray Mckimm, Catherine Shaw, Helena Holrick, Claude and Karen Da Rouche, Lynn Hord, Aaron Pedersen, Lisa Steele, Derek Grantham, Anna Cowie, Tanya Vanzella, Ross Callenberg, Debbie Blott, Suzanne Edwards, Sarah Patterson, Anna Samuelson, Ed Birchmore, the Bellars family, Beth Turner, Nick Haines, Matthew Newnham, Pearl Jordan, Susi Bellamy, Marianne Shillingford and so many more.

Karen Haller is the leading international authority in the field of Applied Colour Psychology – how colour affects and influences our behaviour. With over twenty years of experience, she teaches, consults for businesses, interiors, healthcare and wellbeing; and has worked with prestigious global brands such as Marks and Spencer, Dove and AkzoNobel Dulux. She has also been interviewed for *Cosmopolitan*, *Stylist* and *The Times*, contributed to the *Huffington Post*, and appeared on *London Live* and Channel 4's *Sunday Brunch*.

www.thelittlebookofcolour.com
Instagram: @Karen_Haller_Colour
Twitter: #TheColourRevolution

Photo credits

p. 201   AnjelikaGr / Shutterstock

p. 203   Ayman-Alakhras, iStock / Getty Images

p. 204   p.204 View Pictures / UIG / Getty Images

p. 210-211   Anna Cowie, Art Director, The Pixel Pusher Ltd, UK,
             www.thepixelpusher.co.uk

p.218   Photographee.eu / Shutterstock

p. 226   Photographee.eu / Shutterstock

p. 228   LightField Studios / Shutterstock

p. 229   Photographee.eu / Shutterstock

p. 230   jayk7 / Getty Images

p. 242   S-BELOV / Shutterstock

P.244   alessandro pinto / Shutterstock

p.252   StevanZZ / Shutterstock

p. 260   By Gita Kulinitch Studio / Shutterstock

p. 265   Kristina Gasperas Makeup Artist,
             www.kristinagasperas.com

Your authentic self: a colourful life

Afew years ago, I facilitated in a large colour event for families. The idea was for children and adults to have all sorts of fun and games with colour, to meet scientists and colour experts. There were lots of different things to do and try so as to feel and understand colour in inspiring new ways. Now, the children were all laughing and chattering excitedly and producing these amazing pictures. Even their paint dishes were mini-masterpieces! But the adults were – paralysed. 'What if I get it wrong?' someone said to me. She hesitated even to make a mark with a crayon on a piece of paper.

You have only to look at children playing with colour to see how happy it makes us. But somewhere along the line we can lose that love and spontaneity. We worry about being thought childish or foolish and, fearful of being judged, we hold ourselves back and retreat from colour. Often as we grow up, we leave our authentic selves behind and live out of those parts of ourselves that we believe are more acceptable. We can lose touch with the colours that connect us to ourselves and that make us happy. Before we know where we are, we have disconnected from colour and lost our colour instincts altogether.

My aim in this book has been to reconnect you, to help you to recover that instinctive relationship and to lead you back along the Yellow Brick Road to your authentic self. Colour has profound lessons to teach us about ourselves and who we really are. As you have seen in these pages, it connects us to our memories and experiences, to our cultures and our surroundings, our assumptions, our aspirations, our hopes, wishes and fears, the things we long for and things we wish to escape. Like the Tin Man, the Straw Man and the Lion, we all carry around misconceptions about ourselves. And, like them, we have been on a journey of self-discovery. Reading through this book, you have learnt how to peel back the layers of false self, and to reconnect to who you truly are, to what was there all along, right from the very start.

For me, colour is all about connecting to your true personality. When I talk about living a colourful life, this is what I mean. A colourful life is a state of mind, an attitude. It is a life that is lived from your authentic self, from the essence of who you are, from the inside out, in your own unique style. Living a colourful life is not about going all out with colour. It is about not being afraid to express who you truly are. When we are in touch with who we are through colour, we are connected to what is instinctive and true. And when we are connected to what is instinctive and true, we are on the road to living more authentic, joyful and natural lives.

Riding the crest of the wave: a call to action

The world I want to live in is a world where this is the norm, where everyone uses colour for positive change and wellbeing. Together we can create a global colour revolution, where we embrace colour and know how to harness its positive emotional power.

For this I need your help.

I work with people. I look at behaviour. I am not a scientist, shut away in a laboratory. I take colour into the world, and look for patterns in the way we connect and respond to it. This book is a result of decades of observing people from around the world.

I'm gathering this experiential data to create an innovation paper on the impact of colour in real life and how this can be integrated into environmental and behavioural psychology best practice.

Every one of my consultations is unique as every person has their own personal relationships with colour. Researchers in universities all over the world are working to assess the emotional effects of colour – but nothing is as enlightening as the stories you have to tell about how colour has been and is used in your everyday lives.

Can you contribute to the Colour Revolution by sharing your stories on social media? Send me your colour stories, the charts and diaries so we can collect our own data.

Instagram: @Karen_Haller_Colour #TheColourRevolution
Twitter: @KarenHaller #TheColourRevolution
Facebook: @KarenHallerColourAndDesign #TheColourRevolution

Together we can create the next big step in colour's evolution.

Choose the colours that make you happy

A lot of people think that if you like colour, you have to go all out crazy for it – which is one reason why they pull back from it. But I have shown you that it doesn't need to be full-on kaleidoscopic. We don't need all the colours around us all the time. We can choose what we need, when we need it, to give us the support and everyday happiness we crave. I make sure I have a range of colours in my home and in my wardrobe, so that I can have colour around me or on me when I need it. I never feel the absence of it. I'm conscious of knowing what to look for, with what to surround myself and which colours are the ones that resonate with me.

The exercises and practical tips in this book have been designed to help make you more conscious of your colour choices, to help you to pull colour into every area of your life, to show you where the colour happiness lies so that you never need to feel the absence of it, to show you how to add it in if you feel it's missing, to support you. Now that you have your personal colour palette, and understand the positive and adverse traits of all the main colours, you have

wonderfully individualized tools to transform how you think, how you feel and what you do; they can boost your self-esteem, your self-expression and your happiness – and can give you the correct combination (the secret code) that enables you to flourish and to develop your own very personal relationship with colour.

So off you go. This is only the start of your colour journey, and I have taken you as far as I can for the moment. But you now know what to do and you have seen how easy it is. When you connect to your true self, you can't go wrong. There is no such thing as bad taste. You can't make a mistake. There are no rules except to listen to yourself and follow what you truly love. So trust your instincts and surround yourself with colours that make you feel good and that fill your heart with joy. I look forward to seeing you further down the road at www.thelittlebookofcolour.com. We will continue our colour journey there and change the whole world for the better.

CHAPTER 5
The colour revolution

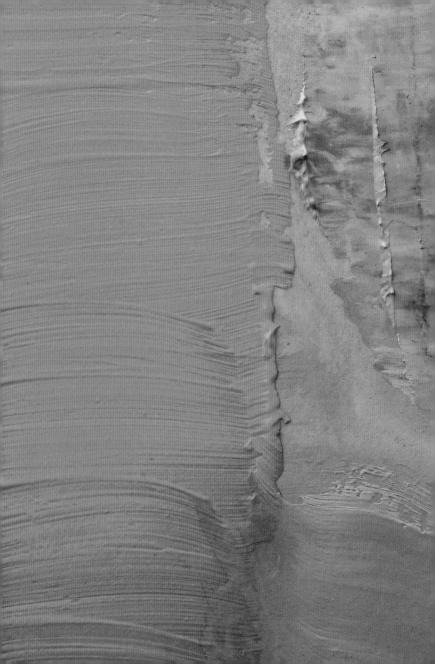